D0947377

Are you free as you are? Are you in any degree bound by your appetites, your passions, your self-will? Are you at all in bondage to the opinion of your neighbors, to the customs and notions of society, however harmful or absurd? These do not trammel the true Shaker.

Eldress Anna White, 1904

Front hall, center family dwelling,
Pleasant Hill, Kentucky.

THE SHAKERS

HANDS TO WORK HEARTS TO GOD

*The History and Visions of the United Society of Believers
in Christ's Second Appearing from 1774 to the Present*

TEXT
Amy Stechler Burns

PHOTOGRAPHS
Ken Burns, Langdon Clay, Jerome Liebling

FOREWORD
Eldress Bertha Lindsay

HISTORICAL PHOTOGRAPHS FROM THE COLLECTIONS OF
*Fruitlands Museum, Harvard, Massachusetts
Hancock Shaker Village, Massachusetts
New York State Museum, Albany
Shaker Museum, Old Chatham, New York
Shaker Village at Canterbury, New Hampshire
United Society of Shakers at Sabbathday Lake, Maine
Henry Francis du Pont Winterthur Museum Library, Delaware*

AN APERTURE BOOK

Shaker chair,
Hancock, Massachusetts.

The peculiar grace of a Shaker chair is due to the fact that it was built by someone capable of believing that an angel might come and sit on it.

Thomas Merton

Group portrait of sisters from Canterbury, New Hampshire, and Sabbathday Lake, Maine.   Although the Shakers
opposed ornament and kept their walls bare of images, they always had an inventive spirit and love of
progress and enjoyed posing for photographs, very carefully presenting themselves to local studio photographers.

AUTHORS' NOTE   Late in the summer of 1981, we drove out of Pittsfield, Massachusetts, west on Route 20, looking for interesting rural architecture, but the road was too well traveled for surprises. Instead it was lined with endless shopping centers, motor inns, and car dealers. Suddenly, we drove into the heart of a perfect, early nineteenth-century village. The buildings were so compelling in their unusual shapes and luminous colors that we pulled off the road and spent the day.

We had found Hancock Shaker Village, one of the restored homes of the American religious group. The Shakers, we learned, lived communally and practiced celibacy and perfectionism. At Hancock there was one dwelling, a five-story brick building that had housed a hundred men and women, a red washhouse, workshops, a meetinghouse, and a perfect, round stone barn—an American cathedral. The buildings were wonderful architecturally, with their intentional proportions and unique dimensions but more than that, they seemed to be suffused with the lives of the people who had lived in them. It was as if the silent rooms and the empty village had a certain aura, a special vibrancy that was much more than the careful combination of wood and brick and glass. Informational placards and pamphlets couldn't begin to explain the mysterious presence that lingered in the village, and we grew passionately interested to know who these people were.

For the next year we read the Shakers' own words and books by scholars, looked at thousands of photographs, and visited the remaining village sites. This research became the foundation of our film, *The Shakers: Hands to Work, Hearts to God,* produced in 1984 for public television. The film has now become the foundation for this book. We have tried to present the Shakers simply, as they were, in the hope of illuminating *who* they were. But the question has no simple answer. The more light we cast on the Shakers, the more fascinating and mysterious they become. *Who are these people?*

Amy Stechler Burns and Ken Burns
Walpole, New Hampshire, 1987

Brother J.J. Randlett, Enfield, New Hampshire.

Brother Augustus Wells Williams, Hancock.

Eldress Anna White, Mount Lebanon, New York.

Eldress Lizzie Noyes, Canterbury.

O the blessed gospel,
O the blessed gospel,
it shall be mine.
I will labor for it,
I will labor for it,
It shall be mine.
            Shaker hymn

Round barn and
poultry house, Hancock.

CONTENTS

Love the inward, new creation,
Love the glory that it brings;
Love to lay a good foundation,
In the line of outward things.
Love a life of true devotion,
Love your lead in outward care;
Love to see all hands in motion,
Love to take your equal share.

Love to love what is belov'd,
Love to hate what is abhorr'd;
Love all earnest souls that covet
Lovely love and its reward.
Love repays the lovely lover,
And in lovely ranks above,
Lovely love shall live forever,
Loving lovely loved love.

                 Shaker hymn

FOREWORD

Eldress Bertha Lindsay, 1986.

My mother and father passed away when I was a young child. They used to visit the Shaker village in Canterbury, New Hampshire, and go to public worship on Sunday, and they loved the Shakers dearly. They decided that if anything happened to them, they wanted me placed here, with the Shakers. So I was brought to Canterbury on May 27, 1905, when I was eight years old. It was apple-blossom time, and we marched down through the orchards and saw the beautiful blossoms and had our service outdoors. That was the first impression I got as a little girl: the beauty of this place and the love I felt from the sisters.

I think I have been really blessed in my life with having been loved greatly. It has been one of the joys of my life, that I have been here and been loved. Being a Shaker has been a privilege. I might have wanted a house of my own, but after all I've only sacrificed my selfish feelings and personal love of some things for something that is much better. The experience of being a Shaker is not only a home to live in, it's a wonderful sense of having everything to make life joyous, and religion should be a joyous experience for people.

We are simple people who believe in Christ. Like good Christians everywhere, if we live by his teachings we are good people and good Shakers. We feel that the Christ spirit comes to each person individually, differently, not at the same time. If the Christ spirit is in my life, then Christ has come. We know that Christ is with us every day.

We were patterned after the early church of the apostles. The Book of Acts speaks of the community that anyone could join. They brought their goods with them, to be shared by all, and each shared in everything that was provided. And so that is the basis of our union and our life in community.

We are celibate, and so we do not marry. We have nothing against marriage, as many people believe. We feel that marriage is a sacred ceremony that should be held sacred. But we feel that we can serve God better singly. If we were married, it would be a selfish kind of life. We would have to tend to our own families, and our husbands and children would come first, no matter what. While we're celibate, we can have a universal love for everyone. We don't have children of our own, but we are very capable of taking care of other people's children. I have taken care of many little girls and have been able to teach them how to live a good Christian life.

Although we kneel down to pray or go separately into a quiet room, we also put that devotion into our daily work and our daily living. In order to have everything as perfect as God made it, we must have perfect devotion to whatever we do. If we live one year, or one day, or a thousand, we want to put the same love into our work as we would if we knew we were going to live forever. Take the meeting-house for an example. When it was built in 1792, it was erected without the sound of a loud word. The builders put all their reverence and devotion into the work. It was an example of the religious life, just put into practice. People love our furniture, they love the simplicity of it, but they also realize that it is the result of a life given to loving people and loving God.

The people who have lived before us, the wonderful, consecrated lives that have been lived here, have, I think, left their impression. We think that it is our mission now, to give that spirit to people as they come here. We don't impose our religion on people, but if we are asked we try to explain what our religion means, and that anyone can live a Shaker life anywhere, because it is very simple: just live by the teachings of Christ and meet everyone in a brotherly spirit with a lot of love, because that is what the world needs today.

It has been prophesied that there would be a renewal of the spirit, but not in community form. And in a way, we feel that it is coming to pass, because so many young people are feeling that spirit and wanting to live a better life. Don't you think that a lot of young people are searching for something that they have not had in their lives? When they come here and feel what we try to give out—the love and the spirit of fellowship to everybody—they seem to want that, and I think it touches their hearts to care about the religious side, something that's different from what they get in their own lives.

While we may have closed our doors to new members, we have never closed our hearts, and we still welcome many young people to talk with us. We feel that we are still witnessing for our church and for God, so nothing is going to be lost.

One of our old singing books says that the songs are made for the day in which they are sung. As the years go by these will change, and you will have other songs to sing. Times change, and we have to accept what comes; keeping up with the times hasn't taken away from our devotion to God. But we don't accept that Shakerism is going to die, ever. The physical aspects of Shakerism may disappear, but the life of dedication will always be here, and the principles of Shakerism will go on forever.

Eldress Bertha Lindsay
Canterbury, New Hampshire
September 2, 1986

Bertha Lindsay, 1909.

Canterbury meetinghouse.   The first meetinghouse was built at New Lebanon in 1785 by
Brother Moses Johnson. His skill as a carpenter and his sense of perfection were prized by the
leadership, and he was sent across New England to build identical buildings at Hancock and Shirley,
Massachusetts, Alfred and Sabbathday Lake, Maine, and Enfield and Canterbury, New Hampshire.

INTRODUCTION

It is as impossible to fully set forth the power and effects of this new religion as to trace the airy road of the meteor.

Valentine Rathbun, 1781

Zaddock Wright lived in Canterbury, New Hampshire, at the start of the Revolutionary War. Unlike his neighbors, he was a royalist and refused to take up arms against the king. According to an early chronicle he fled to Canada "to avoid the dangers to which his political principles exposed him" but was arrested when he returned for his family and thrown into prison in Albany.*

Before his incarceration Zaddock Wright had been deeply affected by the religious revival that, like the Revolution, was sweeping across New England. He was "under great exercise of mind concerning the work of God," and was also "in great tribulation" over his family, his estate, and the Revolution.

At the same time, several cells away, a woman named Ann Lee was being held, accused of treason against the new government. Zaddock knew of her; she was a prophet, the English leader of a tiny radical sect of Christians called the Shakers. Her small group had recently "opened

*All quoted material within the text is drawn from original Shaker sources. See the Selected Bibliography for further information.

their testimony" on the frontier near Albany and ignited a wildfire of disruption and religious fervor.

Zaddock spoke with Mother Ann, as her followers called her, through the grates of his cell, and informed her of his "embarrassments." "You will be delivered," she told him. "God will deliver you." Although this seemed unlikely to Zaddock, the declaration "made a forcible impression upon his feelings." They spoke at length about the Revolution. Ann Lee taught him to "view the subject from a different light than what he had done, and convinced him that it was the providential work of God to open the way for the Gospel." Zaddock agreed that it would be impossible for England to win. "The hand of God was in the Revolution," he wrote, "and America must be separated from the English government and become a land of liberty for the gospel's sake."

Within a year, Zaddock was freed from prison and returned to his family, as Ann Lee predicted. He joined the Shakers and "continued faithful to the end of his days."

· · · · · ·

One afternoon I was at a neighbor's house when two young women attired in Shaker costumes appeared at the rear door. They said the Shakers always lived according to their profession, were honest and upright, but that they did not wish to live a celibate life any longer.

A strange sensation seemed to creep over me, and something like a voice said, "Why listen to them? Go to the Shakers. See for yourself who and what they are."

Eldress Antoinette Doolittle, 1824

They called themselves the United Society of Believers in Christ's Second Appearing, but because of their ecstatic dancing the world called them Shakers.

The Shakers were celibate, they did not marry or bear children, yet theirs is the most enduring religious experiment in American history. Seventy-five years be-

Canterbury meetinghouse. "We think that man cannot hope to attain a spiritual heaven until he first creates a heaven on earth."

Brothers George Clark, left, and Alonzo Hollister. *Opposite, top:* Shaker women at Elijah Wild's house, Shirley. Most Shaker villages began with a house or land donated by an early convert. Brother Elijah Wild's house, the first at Shirley, became the site of brutal mob attacks on Mother Ann during her journey through New England. *Opposite, bottom:* Six Shaker sisters.

fore the emancipation of the slaves and one hundred fifty years before women began voting in America, the Shakers were practicing social, sexual, economic, and spiritual equality for all members.

The Shakers were ordinary people who chose to give up their families, property, and worldly ties in order "to know, by daily experience, the peaceable nature of Christ's kingdom." In return, they were welcomed into "holy families" where men and women lived as brother and sister, where all property was held in common, and where each participated in the rigorous daily task of transforming the earth into heaven.

Shakerism was founded by an illiterate English factory worker named Ann Lee. Guided by divine visions and signs, she and eight pilgrims came to America in 1774 to spread her gospel in the New World.

At their height in 1840 more than six thousand believers lived in nineteen communal villages from New England to Ohio and Kentucky. Tales of their peaceful and prosperous lives impressed the world's utopians. But Shaker aspirations were divine, not social or material. As millennialists, they were unified in the belief that Christ had come again, first in the person of Mother Ann and subsequently "in all in whom the Christ consciousness awakens." It was therefore the duty of each believer to live purely in "the king-

dom come" and to strive for perfection in everything he or she did.

Work was the currency of their service. If the world was to be redeemed and restored to God, the Shakers would accomplish it by the dedicated labor of their hands. They believed that God dwelt in the details of their work and in the quality of their craftsmanship. All their devotion, which no longer went to family or home, was put into what they made. Their villages were meticulously constructed and maintained, their workshops were world renowned for reliable goods, and their gardens provided amply for their own needs, with plenty to spare for the poor.

Shakerism is a system which has a distinct genius, a strong organization, a perfect life of its own, through which it would appear to be helping to shape and guide, in no small measure, the spiritual career of the United States.
Hepworth Dixon, 1867

For more than two hundred years Shakerism ran alongside American history, sometimes heralding things to come, usually reflecting trends, events, and ideals from a slightly different angle. The Shakers arrived in America on the eve of the Revolution, having left England in pursuit of freedom. They were gathered into order as a practicing religion in 1787, just as the new United States found its form with the drafting of the Constitution. That same year Shaker women were officially

given equal rights, and in 1817 the Shakers' southern societies freed the slaves belonging to members and began buying black believers out of slavery. The Shakers were suddenly appreciated as successful communitarians when Americans became interested in communities, as successful utopians when America hosted a hundred utopian experiments, as spiritualists when American parlors filled with mediums and with voices from other worlds. They invented hundreds of laborsaving devices from the clothespin to the circular saw, which they shared without patents (some of these machines launched brilliant industrial careers for the men who borrowed them), nor were they frightened of useful inventions. The New Hampshire Shakers owned one of the first cars in the state and rigged up electricity in their own village

while the state capitol building was still burning gas. They were admired and derided, imitated for their successes and ridiculed for their eccentricities. And they are enduringly appreciated for their contribution to American crafts and architecture.

Today, just a few Shakers still live in a single village in Maine. To all appearances these are the last Shakers. But the living Shakers faithfully assert that their religion will never die. Mother Ann predicted that Shakerism would dwindle to as few members as a child could count on one hand, and then overcome all nations. "This is God's work," says Sister Mildred Barker, "and what could bring that to an end? Nothing that we humans, that mortals do."

If their principles are maintained and sustained by a practical life, it is destined eventually to overthrow all other religions.
Thomas Jefferson, 1808

There is no fear that this, or any other religious sect that is founded altogether on fanaticism and folly, will ever arrive at the smallest importance. James Fenimore Cooper, 1828

· · · · ·

Tens of thousands of people have visited the Shakers over the years. Their impressions have differed vastly, depending on their expectations and on what aspect of Shakerism they happened to encounter.

15

Inevitably their understanding of Shakerism has been partial—limited in direct proportion to what they excluded from their view.

Many people found Shaker life idyllic. They saw pristine and orderly villages with thousands of acres of land, barns full of healthy livestock, and fields burgeoning with grain. They saw workshops filled with gadgets and machinery that turned out a huge volume of salable goods valued for their craftsmanship and durability. They met men and women who lived comfortably, free of material want, free of poverty, crime, and loneliness. They saw sisters in plain dresses and white caps, talking and laughing quietly among themselves as they did dozens of varied and interesting chores. They saw brothers in broad-brimmed Shaker hats working hard in clothes that were washed and mended for them, eating well at tables offering food as plentiful as it was nutritious, being nursed when they were sick, and living free of the uncertainty and burden of supporting a family. Good health and longevity were the rule in Shaker villages.

No Dutch town has a neater aspect, no Moravian hamlet a softer hush. Every building, whatever may be its use, has something of the air of a chapel. The paint is all fresh, the planks are all bright, the windows are all clean, and everything in the hamlet looks and smells

Eldress Sarah Collins taping a Shaker chair, Mount Lebanon.

like household things that have long been laid up in lavender and roseleaves. The people are like their village; soft in speech, demure in bearing, gentle in face; a people seeming to be at peace not only with themselves, but with nature and heaven. Hepworth Dixon

Commonest were the observers who came only on Sunday and knew nothing more of the Shakers than their notorious worship. In the meetinghouse all reverence for order was suspended and the Shakers danced, sang spontaneously, and prayed with unregulated ardor. The shuffling dances that sometimes broke out into wild individual displays horrified visitors to the point of causing some to faint. At times worshipers were seized with "the power of God" as they spoke in tongues or were even hurled, limbs twitching, across the room. Fanny Appleton Longfellow described Shaker worship as "unearthly, revolting, oppressive and bewildering."

Charles Dickens, Nathaniel Hawthorne, Ralph Waldo Emerson, and Presidents Jefferson, Jackson, and Monroe all commented on the Shakers. For the most part they were favorably impressed, though the common attitude among notable men was that the Shakers' "ridiculous religious practices" degraded an otherwise exemplary life. Leo Tolstoy thought that the Shakers could conquer the world if not for their spiritualism. Friederich Engels based

his confidence in communism on the Shakers' example, but he wanted to isolate their social success from the "religious humbug."

A very few observers understood what the Shakers already knew: what met the eye was only the image of a life with a much deeper purpose. Behind the idyllic setting there was a spiritual intent, behind every indication of prosperity there was a sacrifice, behind every freedom there was a submission. At the core of Shakerism stood the belief that the elevation of the spirit was possible only through the discipline of its opposite, the flesh. Daily life was governed by rituals that restricted the body in the hope of freeing the spirit. Relations between the sexes were regulated down to the most minute details. Individual rights were subject to the absolute authority of two elders and two eldresses. Obedience to them was viewed as an op-

Shaker chairs, center family dwelling, Pleasant Hill.
The Shakers lined the walls of dwellings and workshops
with pegs, so that everything could be hung up at night,
for easy cleaning in the morning. The dwelling at Pleasant
Hill has over three thousand hand-turned pegs.

Attic, center family dwelling,
Pleasant Hill.

Bedroom, dwelling, Hancock.   "Do not be expensive or
extravagant in your buildings; but modest and neat.
For a lowly cottage, in order and cleanliness,
is far more beautiful than a grand dwelling."

portunity for Believers to be free of their own passions and appetites. The Shakers' fruitful labor aimed not for products or profit but for perfection. Craftsmen could not sign their work, and jobs were frequently rotated lest Believers forget that their labors were in service to God. Even in their beautiful architecture, form followed function. Every building was designed to be simple, useful, and sound. In contrast, dancing was the Shakers' joy, a "spiritual inspiration" earned by sacrificing the ordinary pleasures of men. It was the union with God and with each other that they had paid for during a week of discipline and denial.

The parts of Shakerism are inseparable from the whole. A way of life that was remarkably sane could look fanatical and frightening when its elements were isolated from each other. But precisely those parts that observers wanted to subtract were responsible for the parts that were held up and admired. The Shakers are enduringly fascinating for their original and successful social order, their industriousness and beautiful products, their benevolence and joyfulness. But to ignore the essential religious purpose, and the celibacy and dance that were the heart of its practice, is to misunderstand the Shakers.

Who were these people? An academic inquiry into a religious people gives a lim-

The Canterbury Quartet.   These four sisters—Helena Sarle, Jennie Fish, Josephine Wilson and Jesse Evans— were known as the Canterbury Quartet and performed Shaker music in public for over 25 years.

Opposite: Upstairs hallway, center family dwelling, Pleasant Hill.   Buildings in the southern villages were not designed to conserve heat, as in New England, but rather to be well ventilated in warm weather. High ceilings and tall doorways were "practical" at Pleasant Hill, and their beautiful effect was secondary.

ited view of their real lives. Even after a sympathetic and comprehensive study of Shakerism, an essential mystery remains. How can a religion be understood, once its practice has virtually ceased and first-hand experiences and impressions are no longer available?

The Shakers embodied their spirit in form. They believed that through their labors the world around them could be perfected and thus redeemed, and so their strivings toward holiness, their gestures toward God, were enacted with their hands. The Shakers dedicated their hearts to God by putting their hands to work. The things that they made don't simply represent but actually *are* their religion in practice. And so first hand experiences and impressions of these people are still available, through the things that they have left behind.

Shakerism can be seen by carefully looking—at buildings and faces, at the light as it falls across a hallway. In ten thousand artifacts, what has passed is still visible. In thousands of photographic images, evidence of the Shakers' genuine aspirations is available to the discerning eye. In villages as they now stand, a true understanding of Shakerism is available, in direct proportion to one's observations.

'Tis a gift to be simple, 'tis a gift to be free,
'Tis a gift to come down where we ought
* to be,*
And when we find ourselves in the place
* just right,*
We'll be in the valley of love and delight.

When true simplicity is gained,
To bow and to bend we'll not be ashamed;
To turn, turn, will be our delight,
Till by turning, turning, we come round right.

Shaker hymn

I have come,
and I've not come in vain.
I have come to sweep
the house of the Lord
clean, clean, for I've come,
and I've not come in vain.
With my broom in my hand,
with my fan and my flail,
this work I will do
and I will not fail,
for lo! I have come
and I've not come in vain.

Shaker hymn

Sister's cloak and
bonnet, Hancock.

1. OPENING THE GOSPEL

And when the time was fully come, according to the appointment of God, Christ was again revealed, not in Judea, to the Jews, nor in the person of a male, but in England, to a gentile nation, and in the person of a female.
Testimonies of the Life, Character, Revelations,
and Doctrines of Mother Ann Lee,
Collected from Living Witnesses, 1816

Ann Lee was born on leap year, February 29, 1736, in Manchester, England. Raised in the slums by a poor blacksmith and his wife, the second of eight children, she worked fourteen-hour days in a factory and never went to school. "She was very illiterate, so that she could neither read nor write." Described as a sensitive child "subject to religious impressions and divine manifestations," she herself once said that the apostles and prophets used to "look after her wishfully, and she wondered at it." Even as a child she was tormented by a sense of her own impurity and "had a great abhorrence of the fleshly co-habitation of the sexes." In 1762 her parents forced her against her conscience to marry Abraham Stanley, a blacksmith like her father. The union was intolerable to her.

I went to bed with my husband but could not sleep seemingly any more than if I had been on a bed of embers. I often rose from my bed at night and walked on the floor in my stocking feet, lest I should stir up his affections, and I was careful not to lay any temptation before him. My husband was opposed to me, and went and complained of me to the church. The church opposed my testimony and tried to persuade me to give it up, but I had to stand the test against my husband, my relations and the church, and I soon received such a power of God that my bed would rock under me and my husband was glad to leave it. Ann Lee

Several years before her marriage Ann Lee had joined a religious sect, an offshoot of the Quaker Church led by a tailor and his wife, James and Jane Wardley. Jane Wardley told Ann, "James and I lodge together, but do not touch each other any more than two babes. You may return and do likewise." The Wardleys preached that the end of the world was at hand, that Christ would soon reign, and that his return would take the form of a woman, as the psalms predicted. They shunned the church and the clergy, had visions, heard voices, and saw signs in the sky. Their worship was influenced by the Camisards, French prophets who had fled to England in the early eighteenth century to escape persecution in France. The Camisards were "despised and derided by almost all classes" for their trances, speeches in tongues, and agitations of the body. These the Wardleys adopted, and their group became known as the "Shaking Quakers" or "Shakers." Their meetings were described as Quakerlike at first:

They would sit in silent meditation for a while, when they were taken with a mighty trembling under which they would express the indignation of God against all sin. At other times they were affected, under the power of God, with a mighty Shaking, and were occasionally exercised in singing, shouting, or walking the floor under the influence of spiritual signs, or swiftly passing and repassing each other like clouds agitated by a mighty wind. Testimonies

For the first eight years of her membership, Ann Lee didn't participate actively but rather used the Wardleys for personal support as her own sufferings grew more and more intense. Despite her protestations, she bore the blacksmith four children. Three died as infants, and the

Second meetinghouse at New Lebanon. On Sundays, the sisters wore white and can be seen here entering the meetinghouse through their door on the right, while the brethren enter on the left.

fourth lived only a few years. The tragedies weakened her body and devastated her heart, but they fortified her conviction that she had "violated God's laws."

Soon after I set out to travel in the way of God, I labored anights continually crying to God for my own redemption. I denied myself every gratification of a carnal nature, of everything which my appetite craved, and ate and drank only that which was mean and poor, that my soul might hunger for nothing but God.

Ann Lee

Ann Lee suffered for nine years. She craved to know "how the creation was fallen, and how the restoration should take place." One of her devoted attendants wrote that "for whole nights together her cries, screeches and groans were such as to fill every living soul around her with fear and trembling." She was sometimes "in such extreme agony of soul as to cause the blood to perspire through the pores of her skin."

But she did receive "gifts," infrequent periods of peace when visions and understandings would come to her. Once, after a twelve-day vigil, she said, "I saw the Lord Jesus in his kingdom and glory. He revealed to me the depth of man's loss and that sin which is the root of all evil; the doleful works of the flesh. And I felt the power of God flow into my soul like a fountain of living water." And then she would again be enveloped in her anguish. Shaker biographers liken her suffering to Christ's sojourn in the wilderness or Muhammad's in Arabia—the price other inspired leaders paid for their understanding.

I served God day and night and cried for deliverance from all sin. I did not receive a gift of God and then go away and think it was

sufficient without travelling any further. I labored to feel a sense of the sufferings and torments of hell, that I might keep my soul continually awake to God. Ann Lee

Soon after the death of her fourth child, Ann Lee joined the Wardleys with full conviction and began to testify in public. The group's visibility increased, and so did their membership. Their outspoken condemnation of marriage and the church, and their warnings to all who participated in either institution, began to arouse suspicion and violence. The Shakers sometimes met all night long, their loud and frenzied worship alarming the neighborhood. Twice the town constable had to use force to disperse a mob outside a Shaker meeting, and Shakers were thrown in jail for "breach of the Sabbath." Several times Ann Lee and others were arrested for "going into Christ Church in Manchester and there willfully and contemptuously, in the time of divine service, disturbing the congregation then assembled at morning prayers."

I bore testimony against their sins, and told them of their wicked lives, which was the reason of their hating me so. Ann Lee

Violence against the Shakers increased. They were stoned and beaten and dragged through the streets.

I suffered great persecutions in England on account of my faith. Sometimes the power of God operated so mightily upon me that numbers would try to hold me still, but the more they tried to withstand the power of God, the more I was operated upon. One, being greatly enraged, said he was determined to overcome me. He then beat me over the face and nose with his staff, but I sensibly felt and saw the bright

rays of the glory of God pass between my face and his staff, which shielded the blows so that I did just but feel them. Ann Lee

Finally, in 1772, Ann Lee was put in prison, in a stone cell so small that she couldn't stand. The constable's incomplete account records a two-day stay, but the Shaker legend is quite different: Ann Lee was detained for fourteen days without food or drink, presumably to die in her cell. Instead, a young follower slipped into the prison courtyard each night with a long-stemmed pipe hidden in his coat and fed her a mixture of milk and wine through the keyhole. When at last the door was opened, her jailers were stunned to see her stand without assistance and walk away.

The world were astonished at it, and said that it must be a supernatural power that attended her; and they did not believe it was right to confine or oppress her. Testimonies

Ann Lee's strength as she left prison had come not only from milk and wine, she said. During her incarceration, she told the Wardleys, she had seen Christ in a resplendent vision and had at last understood the full nature of the fall and the possibility of redemption. "I converse with Christ," she told them. "I feel Him present with me as sensibly as I feel my hands together. It is not I that speaks; it is Christ that dwells in me." She told them that the Christ spirit would dwell in any Believer who ceased to commit sin. "If you are saved by Christ, it must be by walking as He walked. And if you have committed sins, you must confess them to those witnesses in whom Christ has taken up his abode. You must forsake the marriage of the flesh, or you cannot be married to the lamb, nor have any share in the resurrection of Christ; for those who are counted worthy neither marry nor are given in marriage, but are like unto the angels."

The Wardleys embraced her vision, her testimony, and her ascendancy to leadership of the sect. She had fulfilled their prophecy of Christ's return in a woman's form, and she became their guide and teacher, Mother Ann.

A feminine church had now been openly proclaimed. Christ had come again, not in his pomp and power as the world expected Him, but in the flesh of a factory girl who could neither read nor write.   Hepworth Dixon

Sometime in 1774, Mother Ann and her followers began to have visions of America, the new land of religious freedom. James Whittaker, the young man said to have fed Mother Ann through the pipe stem, crystallized the image: "I saw a large tree, every leaf thereof shone with a brightness as made it appear like a burning torch, representing the church of Christ which will yet be established in this land." Mother Ann elaborated his prophecy with several of her own. "I knew that God had a chosen people in America. I saw them in a vision, and when I met with them in America, I knew them."

In the summer of 1774 Mother Ann and eight Shakers boarded the *Mariah*, bound for New York. It was not an easy voyage. The *Mariah* had been condemned as unfit to sail before it left England. "God would not condemn it when we were in it," Mother Ann insisted.

"When we were on the water, I was constrained to testify against the wickedness of the seamen, for which they threatened to throw me overboard." Mother Ann led the Shakers in their demonstrative worship anyway. During a storm the ship sprang a leak because of a loose plank "and the water flowed in so rapidly that the captain was greatly alarmed and turned as pale as a corpse." Mother Ann told him of a bright angel sitting by the mast who promised that they would arrive safely in America. Immediately afterward, according to Shaker legend, a huge wave slapped the plank back into place, and they continued safely on their journey. "We have since been informed that the captain said if it had not been for us, he should have been sunk in the sea, and never reached America again; and that he should not be afraid to sail through hell gate with us."

Wherever Mother Ann went, she left in her wake bewildered and sometimes transformed onlookers. Her deportment, her prophecies, and the uncanny series of occurrences that accompanied her were an undeniable statement of power and undid much of the skepticism and ridicule that her strange practices drew. Her ability to convince and convert those she came into contact with became a fundamental factor in the spread of her new religion. Testament to this is the fact that among those closest followers who accompanied her to America were her spurned husband, her scornful father, her brother, her niece, and a man of some wealth who paid the entire passage.

They arrived in New York without a plan and proceeded according to bursts of inspiration and guidance from Ann Lee. At one point she marched the whole group to the doorstep of a house on Pearl Street, addressed the matron of the house by her full name, though she had never seen or heard of her before, and said that God had bid that she accommodate them. The woman did so, graciously.

MOTHER ANN'S APHORISMS

Labor to make the way of God your own. Let it be your inheritance, your treasure, your occupation, your daily calling.

Be faithful with your hands, that you may have something to give the poor.

You must not lose one moment of time, for you have none to spare.

Bring strength to your church, not weakness.

Never have one hard feeling towards each other, but live together every day as though it was the last you had to live in this world.

Arm yourself with meekness and patience.

Just in proportion as you heed the cries of the needy, God will heed yours.

If you improve in one talent, God will give you more.

Quell the spirit of fault finding; do not complain of the way of God until you have proved it; none ever thought it hard who were really in it.

Let your words be few, and seasoned with grace.

Clean your room well, for good spirits will not live where there is dirt. There is no dirt in heaven.

Meetingroom, center family dwelling,
Pleasant Hill.

For most of a year each Shaker found his or her own way in New York, taking work as laborers or servants. For Mother Ann it was a time of increased hardship. Her husband was "visited with a severe sickness," and while she nursed him they had no income at all. On his recovery he began "associating with the wicked," finally insisting again that she "live with him in the flesh and bear children." This was their final break, and she was left alone in the city. "Her labor and travel of soul for the opening of the gospel was often so great," wrote a follower, "as to banish all other concerns. Hence poverty, privation and hunger were her frequent companions."

Three of her followers—John Hocknell, the man of wealth; William Lee, her brother; and James Whittaker—moved north in search of affordable land. They rented a farm in the swampy wilderness of Niskeyuna, New York, near Albany, and after returning to England for money and his family, Hocknell purchased the site that would become the first Shaker village. By early the next year the Shakers were reassembled in a tiny log cabin in the deep forest of the American frontier.

The practical liberty of America is found in its great space and small population. Good land, everywhere available if you will go for it. Laborers from every country in Europe are attracted to it. They come, they toil, they prosper. This is the real liberty of America.
George Flower, 1817

Iroquois Indians and scattered white settlers hardly fulfilled the vision of "great numbers of God's chosen people" that Mother Ann had confidently expected, but the area nonetheless was a perfect place to plant the seed of her teaching. In the 1730s and '40s the region, called the "burnt-over district," had undergone a massive religious revival, the Great Awakening, which had left a sentiment of radical, anticlerical fervor among the populace. Then in the wake of the Revolution came a vast migration of people to the frontier, where the overwhelming hardship of life, the seemingly random ruin, illness, and death, the constant confrontations with the most basic questions of survival, made equally pressing the question of the soul's salvation. Settlers who were daily reminded of their own mortality found it difficult to repress their fear of eternal damnation. Out of this climate burst a second religious revival in the towns near the Shakers' settlement.

The "New Light" revival that began in 1778 was similar in style to the Shakers' own charismatic worship. The New Light Baptists held nightly gatherings with wild preaching, prophecies, and visions, and they awaited Christ's kingdom on earth, which they felt was "near at hand." When Christ had still not returned in 1779, their fervor began to dissipate and the "extraordinary operations ceased." This large group "continued to come together as best they could," a Shaker reported, "to keep their faith and be not discouraged, tho their meetings seemed powerless and heavy." They were prepared and anxious for "further light."

On May 19, 1780, the sun did not rise in the Northeast. It was the ominous, terrifying sign that thousands of rural revivalists had awaited. "The day was as dark as night," wrote a Shaker who witnessed it. "No work could be done in any house without a candle. The people were out wringing their hands and howling, 'the day of judgement is come,' for darkness covered the whole face of New England." On this day the Shakers finally opened their gospel in America, "and that made it darker yet. On the part of the Shakers it was singing, dancing, shouting, shaking, speaking with tongues, preaching, prophesying and warning the world to confess their sins and turn to God, for his wrath was coming upon them." Their performance was electrifying. "We are the people," claimed the Shakers, "who turn the world upside down."

I saw a Shaker woman who was under great operations of the power of God. She shook and trembled mightily, and was carried here and there, and shook till her hair was thrown everyway. I felt struck. I was afraid it was the way of God, and that I would have to embrace it or never find salvation. I thought it would be very abasing to look like that woman. Many embraced the testimony during that summer, and the more I saw them, the more I felt convicted that it was the way of God, and I felt a sting of conscience that I cannot well describe. Sister Hannah Chauncey, 1780

The Shakers received many hundreds of people at Niskeyuna in the months following the "dark day." Some came from the revivals, full of hope that an enduring inspiration rested with the Shakers. Most who came were drawn by a longing that they could not resist, yet filled with dread at what these strange people might require of them. "If I could have believed it would have answered the same purpose, to lay my head down upon a rock and have it cut off," said one convert, "I would rather have done it, the cross seemed so great." But then they met Mother Ann.

Shakers at Watervliet, New York, which was originally called Niskeyuna.

When I arrived, Mother Ann took hold of my hand and led me into the house. She sat down in a chair, and I sat by her side. Her eyes were shut and it appeared that her sense was withdrawn from the things of time. The graceful motion of her hands, the beautiful appearance of her countenance, and the heavenly melody of her voice made her seem like a glorious inhabitant of the heavenly world singing praises to God. As I sat by the side of her, one of her hands frequently touched my arm, and I instantly felt the power of God run through my whole body. Sister Thankful Barce, 1780

The numbers of families, congregations, and towns losing members to the Shakers began to grow, as did widespread alarm.

Those who often saw frenzied women "whirling" along the public road for long distances, and dancing with rhythmic shaking of heads, hands and arms dignified into a ceremonial of worship, were tempted to jeering comment and ridicule; and when they saw happy homes broken up, families impoverished, the acutely nervous made insane, affianced girls frightened into rejection of their sweethearts, it is hardly to be thought strange that sometimes in wrath they sought to scourge out of town the promoters of such distractions.

Henry Stedman Norse, 1894

Mobs began to collect outside their services, Shakers were detained as they did business, and broadsides publicly defamed them:

They meet together and have been heard two miles by people in the dead of night, they run about in the woods and elsewhere hooting and tooting like owls; some of them have stripped naked in the woods and thought they were angels and invisible. Valentine Rathbun, 1781

In revolutionary America, there was ample reason to suspect the Shakers. Their leaders were English, and they preached pacifism at a time when every patriot was taking up arms against the crown.

When any person goes to them to be instructed they inquire of him whether he has given his vote and money for the defense of the country. And presently they tell him it is contrary to the gospel to bear arms; saying Christ's kingdom is not of this world; they labor to convince him that it is a great error to have anything to do with war and fighting.

Valentine Rathbun

In the summer of 1780 Mother Ann was accused of treason and put in prison in Albany. As in England, her incarceration had the unintended effect of arousing sympathy by the unfairness of the charge, increasing her fame, and drawing people to her. She was finally personally released by George Clinton, the first governor of New York. The flow of visitors to Niskeyuna increased.

A poor uneducated factory worker has confounded the wisdom of all men; reformers, legislators and scholars, who have come to nothing as promoters of human happiness.

Elder Frederick Evans, 1888

After a year of "gathering souls" at Niskeyuna, Mother Ann explained to her followers that she now had different work to do. The faces that she had seen so clearly in her English vision were still at large, and she was going to find them. In May 1781, Mother Ann and her closest followers set out on a missionary journey that ignited Shakerism like a chain of bonfires across New England and established in thirty-six towns the converts who would eventually gather to build a dozen Shaker villages.

At Harvard, Massachusetts, they purchased a headquarters, The Square House, built by a self-styled prophet named Shadrack Ireland. Ireland had recently died, and when he failed to be resurrected

Shaker stove,
meetinghouse, Hancock.

Upstairs hallway, meetinghouse,
Sabbathday Lake.

Meetinghouse, Sabbathday Lake. The ground level consisted
of one large room for worship and was lined with built-in benches.

on the third day, as he had promised, he left behind a large, disillusioned following. These people welcomed the Shakers, and Mother Ann settled herself in the midst of a populace ripe for her teaching.

Here Mother Ann found the place and the people which had been shown to her in a vision, and during her residence in this place the gospel had a rapid and extensive circulation. They were visited from almost every quarter of the land where the sound of the testimony had extended. Elder Thomas Hammond, 1853

For two years Mother Ann traveled on foot along paths blazed by revivalist preachers, attracting crowds that had been left desperate for salvation and were eager to hear the new testimony. Her message was simple and radical. "Carnal affections must die," she said, "that spiritual affections may live, for it is impossible that both have an abiding residence in the soul." She testified that the spirit of Christ dwelt in her, and that it might dwell in any who gave up sin. "Put your hands to work, and your hearts to God," she taught them. She urged them to strive for perfection in their work and in their lives, for the millennium had come, and the earth, by their labors, must be redeemed.

She frequently moves from town to town, and constantly sends forth "laborers" as she calls them, to preach and teach her religion to the world. In some towns, mobs have abused and insulted them. This they call persecution, and a proof of their being the true religion which is not part of this world.
William Plumer, 1782

Hundreds of pages of Shaker testimony detail the brutal persecution that followed them across New England. They were whipped and beaten and kidnaped. Mobs dragged them from houses, tied them behind horses, and ran them out of town. Often the local authorities were at the lead. In Petersham, Massachusetts, a mob with firebrands seized Mother Ann and "inhumanly dragged her, feet foremost, out of the house, and threw her into a sleigh with as little ceremony as they would the dead carcass of a beast."

It really seemed as if my life must go from me, when they dragged me out of my room and threw me into the sleigh. Besides they tore my handkerchief from my neck, my cap and fillet from my head, and even tore some of the hair out of my head. Ann Lee

"Their pretense was to find out whether she was a woman or not." That same evening a mob so nearly killed James Whittaker that they frightened themselves and returned to Mother Ann with a signed agreement that the Shakers "might thereafter pass through the town peaceably." In Shirley, Massachusetts, a deaf man who claimed that the Shakers had stolen his wife gathered a mob that tied a Shaker man to a tree and beat him "until his back was all in a gore of blood and the flesh bruised to a jelly." At Harvard, "a mob of 400 broke into the Square House and dragged out the Shakers. For a distance of seven miles it was one scene of cruelty and abuse, pounding and beating, and pushing off from bridges into the water; every kind of abuse they could invent without taking lives."

So it has been with me ever since I left Niskeyuna, day and night, I have been like a dying creature. Ann Lee

•   •   •   •   •

After I have done my work in this world, there will be a great increase in the gospel. Souls will embrace it by hundreds and by thousands. You will see peaceable times, and you may worship God under your own vine and fig trees. But I shall not live to see it. Ann Lee

The missionary journey was completed at the end of 1783, and the Shakers returned to Niskeyuna. In two years Mother Ann had converted thousands of people, who patiently awaited the time when the Shakers would be "gathered into order." The trip was successful, but Mother Ann, having suffered a fractured skull along the way, was fatally weakened. On September 8, 1784, John Hocknell wrote that he saw Mother Ann "wafted away on a golden chariot." She was just forty-eight years old when she died.

Though Mother's words were generally few, they were always adapted to the occasion; and it did not appear that she ever spoke in vain. So great and God-like was the power of her spirit that with a few words she would instantly raise a whole assembly from a state of deepest tribulation and distress of soul, to a state of most heavenly joy and comfort. Her countenance was mild and lovely, yet grave and solemn. In reproof she was terrible; in admonition she was quick, sharp and powerful as lightning. When she rejoiced, her joy was unspeakable, and it seemed as if her whole soul was with the angelic host. When she wept, it seemed enough to melt a heart of stone. In her manners she was meek, harmless and inoffensive. Her love and charity seemed boundless. When someone kneeled down to her, she often used to say, "Don't kneel to me, kneel to God; I am but your fellow servant." Testimonies

Meetingroom, dwelling, Hancock.   The Shakers made their own stoves for use
in almost every room and for sale to the world's people. As with most
Shaker products, the stoves were the best on the market and could be ordered with
more than two hundred variations. They were designed in the villages, but
uncharacteristically, the stoves were actually cast by local foundries.

Canterbury meetinghouse.

2. GATHERING INTO ORDER

Build me a house, saith the Lord,
And let every heart contribute
As you raise it to My Spirit.
With My Glory I will fill it
And My Power shall be round about.
Let the wise who have long known My Way
Bring these gifts:
Holiness of heart, holiness of life.
Let the young bring their best
To be inwrought for me.
And ye shall all together write:
Holiness, Holiness, Holiness to the Lord God,
Holiness upon all things in His house forever!
Shaker hymn

"Shakerism," at Ann Lee's death, was a group of people scattered over a thousand miles, united by religious conviction, their common acquaintance with Mother Ann, and little more. It had no theology, no daily practice, no home. Across the Northeast, converts feared that Mother Ann would take Shakerism with her to the grave.

But a handful of her closest followers were prepared to create the form in which Shakerism could live. They began tangibly, with a building. At New Lebanon (later called Mount Lebanon), New York, in 1785, James Whittaker ordered the construction of a meetinghouse. It was a small, squat building rooted firmly to the ground and built defiantly to last forever.

Its design contained clear statements of spiritual intentions. Starkly simple, it was built for order and use, without superfluity or decoration. Constructed with care in every seam and joint, it reflected the Shakers' millennial dream of heaven on earth. Symmetrical, with a side for men and a side for women, it represented and reinforced the separate and equal status of the sexes. It was the center of what would become the central village, a magnet for the scattered Believers and a home for the inspiration that Ann Lee left behind. It also became a model for ten identical buildings to be constructed at village sites across New England. "And they shall come from the east and from the west, from the north and from the south, from all nations and hear the gospel in this house," Whittaker said at the building's dedication.

Ye shall come in and go out of this house in reverence and Godly fear. All men shall come in and go out at the west doors, and women at the east doors. There shall be no whispering, talking or laughing, for it was built to worship God in, and to repent in.
James Whittaker, 1786

Shortly after the completion of the New Lebanon meetinghouse, James Whittaker died. To the alarmed Believers who attended his deathbed he said, "I leave them with you who are able to teach you the way of God. We have given you the gospel; see to it that you make good use of it." With his death passed the last of the English leadership. The future of Shakerism was left entirely in American hands.

Original covenant signatures, Watervliet, 1839. When a novitiate was ready to join the Shakers, he or she signed the covenant, yielding up personal possessions and independence, and gaining the full rights and privileges of a Shaker.

. . . . .

It will not be my lot, nor any that came with me from England, to gather and build up the church; but it will be the lot of Joseph Meacham, my first born son in America; he will gather the church into order, but I will not live to see it.   Ann Lee

Joseph Meacham was a New Light preacher who had come to Mother Ann on the "dark day" in 1780. She called him "the wisest man born of a woman in 600 years." At James Whittaker's funeral, Meacham spoke "with such power that it appeared marvelous." But the following day, when the Shakers gathered to await a sign from God indicating who should become their next leader, Joseph Meacham remained silent. Throughout the day the candidates spoke, but no sign came. At last the voice of an anonymous young man was heard, "calm and decided, declaring with a power that left not a shadow of a doubt on the mind of any present, that the silent listener, Joseph Meacham, was the anointed of God to lead his people."

Over the next ten years Joseph Meacham—"Father Joseph"—gave the Shaker religion its form. It would be communal, practiced in small villages separated from the world. Members would jointly own everything and privately own nothing. They would give up their homes and farms and withdraw into communities isolated from the practices and temptations of the world. Celibacy would be a way of life, institutionalized into the social structure, the government, and the architecture. Obedience to the leadership would insure the union of the membership, and daily manual labor would put their religious principles into practice, as well as provide support for the community. Meacham created a daily ritual, a protocol

for meals and for work and for bedtime. He standardized the layout of the villages and the design of the buildings, the forms of worship, and of exchange between the sexes and with the world. "To each act and step," it was said, "he joined a thought of its use."

His first step was monumental—the appointing of a woman, Lucy Wright, to leadership "in the female line." It was said that when Mother Ann first laid eyes on Lucy Wright she smiled and said, "We must save Lucy if we can, for if we save her, it will be equal to saving a nation." With her appointment Meacham formally equalized the sexes and enacted Mother Ann's fundamental assertion of the duality of God.

In 1787 Joseph and Lucy sent word to the scattered Believers that any who were prepared to leave their families and separate themselves from the world should gather at New Lebanon. During the fall converts filled the cabins, barns, and houses that had been dedicated to the new village. On Christmas Day they shared their first meal. It was the beginning of the first Shaker village.

One horse, one wagon, two cows, 27 sheep, 130 pounds of tobacco, one axe, one saddle, one pound of pork, one bed and bedding, four turkeys, two chains and sixteen dollars in money. The above account is what I brought with me when I came to the church.

Brother Peter Ayers, 1787

Opposite: Shaker men and women.
Left: Canterbury meetinghouse. "The raising of the meetinghouse at Harvard was accomplished in one night, that time being chosen so that the eyes of the world might not look upon the event which was considered a sacred rite."
Right: Title page, Father Joseph Meacham's "Concise Principles," 1790. This book represents the first formulation of Shaker theology, and was also the first Shaker book ever published.

A CONCISE STATEMENT OF THE PRINCIPLES OF THE ONLY TRUE CHURCH, ACCORDING TO THE GOSPEL OF THE PRESENT APPEARANCE OF CHRIST. As held to and practised upon by the true followers of the LIVING SAVIOUR, at NEWLEBANON, &c.

TOGETHER WITH A LETTER FROM JAMES WHITTAKER, Minister of the Gospel in this day of CHRIST's second appearing—to his natural relations in England. Dated October 9th, 1785.

Printed at Bennington, Vermont, By HASWELL & RUSSELL—1790.

Converts collected by the hundreds at New Lebanon and several other centers in Maine, New Hampshire, Massachussetts, and Connecticut. Whatever they could bring was accepted, and whatever they needed was provided, as best the community could. They signed the covenant, entering into a "joint interest and union." Husbands and wives became brothers and sisters in "holy families," and children went into their own order. Equality extended across every aspect of communal life. Everyone was fed equally, clothed equally, housed equally. Everyone worked equally and prayed equally.

The time is come for you to give up yourselves and your all to God, to possess as though you possessed not. We shall have one meeting together which will never break up.

Father Joseph Meacham

With the withdrawal of converts from their lives and the world, Shakerism itself also withdrew from the public eye. For ten years, as Meacham struggled to establish a series of villages "in gospel order," all Shaker evangelism ceased and visitors were no longer permitted. The Shakers energy turned inward, toward the development of a practical religion.

Joseph Meacham's system covered nearly every aspect of life: he organized a government, in which two elders and two eldresses would be appointed by the central ministry in New Lebanon to govern each village and a pair of deacons and deaconesses would manage all trade and interchange with the world; he wrote a theology, *A Concise History of the Principles of the Only True Church*, in which a theoretical foundation for the religion was finally articulated in print; and he issued instructions for dress "in plain and modest apparel, but clean and decent according to [the believer's] order and calling, and suitable to their employ," for the education of children, regarding health and doctors, and regarding language, books, and all exchanges with the world.

Meacham traveled continually, gathering Believers into eleven communities. To the deacons assigned to oversee the construction of the villages, Meacham stressed that "order and use" should be their guide. "All work in the church ought to be done plain and decent. . . .Lay out the order of buildings and see that the foundations are well laid, see that the materials for buildings are suitable for their use, and that the work is done in due order." To lay the spiritual foundation of the religion, Meacham instructed Believers "to labor down into mortification deeper than would ever be necessary again." Rigorous introspection and denial were fundamental elements of a strong beginning, Meacham insisted.

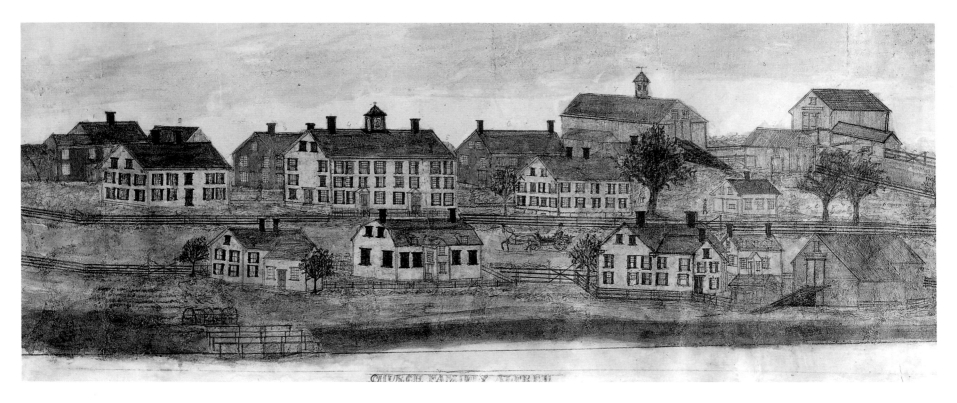

CHURCH FAMILY ALFRED

We were constantly urged to labor in mortification, self-abasement, to think we were almost good for nothing and never would be worth but little. This was depressing, especially to children, but necessary to lay the foundations as deep as any souls would ever be required to travel. Elder Calvin Green, 1823

The previously spontaneous worship was most radically formalized. The wild, individual dances that characterized Mother Ann's decade were almost entirely replaced by orderly, rehearsed rituals that were "received" by Father Joseph and then taught to the people. He was said to have had no natural ability in the dances, but he practiced them so vigorously in a vacant room above a shop that he wore the floor-boards smooth.

By 1796 there were Shaker villages established in New Lebanon and Niskeyuna (now called Watervliet), New York; in Hancock, Harvard, Shirley, and Tyring-ham, Massachusetts; in Enfield, Connecticut; in Canterbury and Enfield, New Hampshire; and in Alfred and Sabbathday Lake, Maine. The villages maintained themselves through the industry implied in Mother Ann's admonition "put your hands to work." At New Lebanon alone the Shakers operated a tannery, a chair factory, a blacksmith shop, a spinning, dyeing, and weaving shop, and a garden-seed industry. Among other crops, the village produced in one year over three thousand bushels of potatoes.

In ten years, while their testimony had been withdrawn from the world, Shakerism was formalized, organized, and set on a path towards prosperity. In the world's eyes it had become productive, peaceful, and almost respectable. The Shaker's worship no longer seemed so threatening, their villages were attractive and orderly, and their salesmen, out on the country roads, sold goods that were rapidly renowned for their high quality and fair price.

They themselves are plain, decent, and grave in their dress, language and deportment. As to integrity, their character is established among all considerate people in this quarter. The contortions, grimaces, and promiscuous dancings which marked and disgraced their conduct when they first arose among us have given way to a mode of worship which tends to inspire sentiments of solemnity rather than derision.
Theological Magazine, 1796

A ministration ceased, and persecution ceased also; and the believers worshipped God in their appointed habitations, unmolested by the wicked. Testimonies

That year, 1796, Joseph Meacham died. He had brought form and structure to Mother Ann's faith. At the end of its second decade, unified and centralized, Shakerism was once again opened to the world.

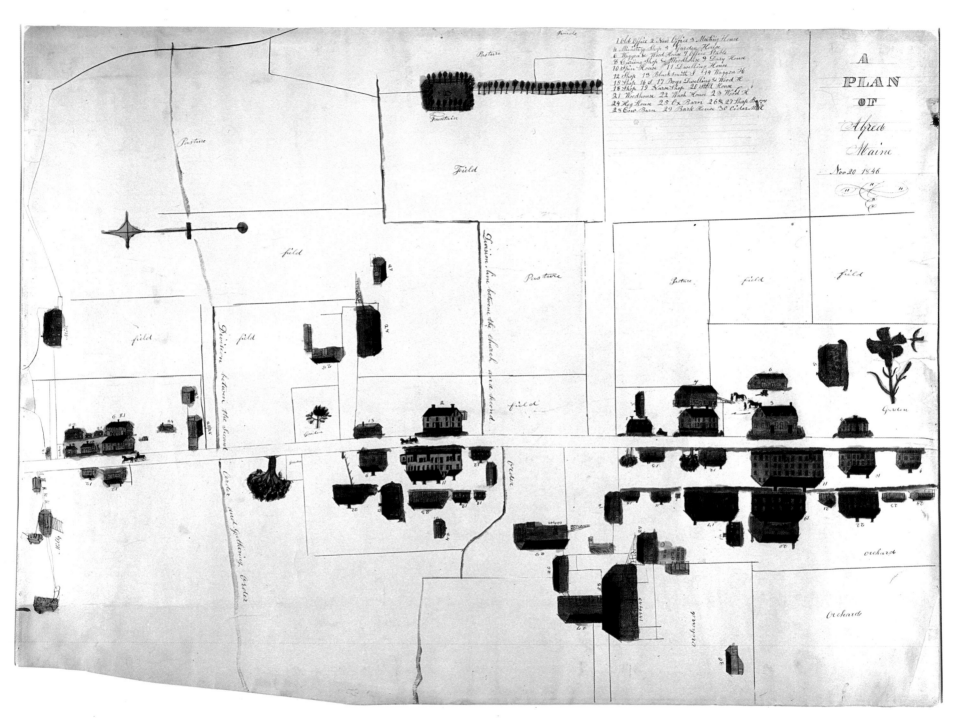

Shaker map of Alfred, Maine.

Opposite, left: Painting of the community at Alfred, November 20, 1846.
At its peak, each Shaker "family" had about one hundred members. If the
population grew much beyond that, a new family within the village was created.
A large village might have three or four branches: center family, second family, north
family, and so on. Each family was self-sufficient with its own dwelling and workshops.

The first people in America, and actually the world, to create a society on the basis of common property are the so-called Shakers. Although their religious practices, and especially the prohibition of marriage, frightened many away, they have nevertheless found a following, and now have eleven large communities, each three to eight hundred strong.

Friederich Engels, 1845

They are an orderly, industrious sect, and models of decency, cleanliness, and of morality too, so far as the human eye can penetrate. I have never seen, in any country, villages so neat and so perfectly beautiful as to order and arrangement, without, however, being picturesque and ornamented as those of the Shakers. James Fenimore Cooper, 1828

The earth does not show more flourishing fields, gardens and orchards than theirs. The finish of every material thing testifies to their wealth both of material and leisure. . . . If such external provision is the result of co-operation and community of property among an ignorant, conceited, inert society like this, what might not the same principles of association achieve among a more intelligent set of people, stimulated by education and exhilarated by the enjoyment of all the blessings that God has placed within the reach of man?

Harriet Martineau, 1837

They inform you that they wish to represent "heaven on earth." Their vow is celibacy, and they have everything in common. How they manage with their combs and toothbrushes, I did not presume to ask.

Archibald Maxwell, 1841

Washhouse, Hancock.   "Simple utility is the only rule of architecture. There is not, in the whole village, one line of ornament."

Opposite, top: Mount Lebanon. The Shaker community at New Lebanon, founded in 1787, changed its name in the 1860s to Mount Lebanon to distinguish itself from the township. It was the central ministry from which all of the Shaker societies were run.

Opposite, bottom: General view of Canterbury village.

Pleasant Hill.

3. THE KENTUCKY REVIVAL

The next opening of the gospel will be in the Southwest. It will be at a great distance, and there will be a great work of God.

Mother Ann

The inhabitants of Kentucky eagerly recommend to strangers the country they inhabit as the best part of the United States, as that where the soil is most fertile, the climate most salubrious, and where all the inhabitants were brought through the love of liberty and independence. The spirit of religion has acquired a fresh degree of strength among the country inhabitants. F.A. Michaux, 1802

In 1800 Kentucky was the Far West, and the same frontier conditions that existed in Niskeyuna twenty years earlier helped two itinerant preachers start a religious revival that "turned Kentucky upside down." These revivalists believed that individuals could receive "New Light" themselves, without the burden of church doctrine. Frontier families worshiped in fields and tents, and in makeshift churches made of timber and mud.

August 6, 1801. Mass meeting. 10,000 to 25,000 people. The noise of the crowd was like the roar of Niagara. Some of the people were singing, others praying, some crying for mercy. I saw at least 500 swept down in a moment as if a battery of a thousand guns had been opened upon them, and then immediately followed shrieks and shouts that rent the heavens. Itinerant preacher

To see these proud young gentlemen and ladies dressed in their silks and jewelry take the jerks.

The first jerk you would see their fine bonnets, caps and combs fly and so sudden would be the jerking of the head that their long loose hair would crack as loud as the wagonner's whip.
Peter Cartwright, 1801

With a characteristic ability to recognize situations and locations ripe for their testimony, the Shaker leadership at New Lebanon dispatched three missionaries to Kentucky. The men walked 1,233 miles in two months and twenty-two days.

Like God's hunters we went through this wild, wooden world, hunting up every soul that God had been preparing for eternal life. The people sucked in our light as greedily as ever an ox drank water, and all wondered where they had been and not seen these things before.
Brother Issachar Bates

The missionaries traveled from farm to farm and mass meeting to mass meeting. At one homestead where they stopped to buy salt, Tobias Wilhite and his wife noted that the Shakers knelt before and after their meal. This simple gesture so impressed the host and hostess that they converted. "Thank the God of heaven that salvation is come!" one revivalist wrote. "Here goes wife and child, houses and land for the kingdom of heavens sake." Many of the leaders of the revival also joined, bringing large congregations with them. Richard

McNemar wrote that these strangers were in "actual possession of that salvation" which the hysteria of the revival failed to produce, and offered a way of life that was "no mere speculation" but "had been for many years reduced to practice and established by the living experience of hundreds."

For upwards of 15 years my soul has been on a wheel, forming into union with professed followers of the lamb, but never did I find my mate until I found the spirit from New Lebanon. Elder Richard McNemar

Center family dwelling, Pleasant Hill.

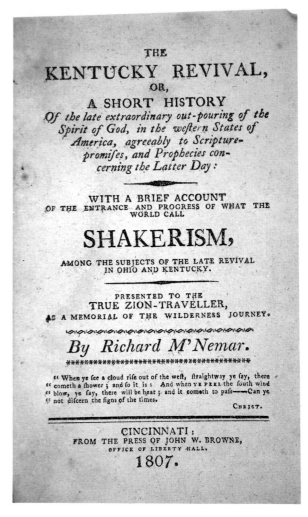

Left: Center family dwelling at Pleasant Hill with Shakers along the fence.
Right: Title page, Elder Richard McNemar's history, *The Kentucky Revival*.

Other revivalists choked on celibacy, or resented being upstaged by strangers. The very powerful Reverend Barton Stone "was never so completely swallowed up with any man than as with Issachar Bates while he opened the testimony . . . until they came upon marriage." "He set more store by his wife Eliza," Brother Issachar said of Stone, "than by all the salvation that God had prepared for the fallen race."

They have made shipwreck of faith and turned aside to an old woman's fables. These wolves in sheep's clothes have smelt us from afar and have come to tear, rend and devour.

Rev. Barton Stone, 1805

Another preacher, John Thompson, charged that "the false prophets and liars were parting man and wife, breaking up families and churches, and taking away people's lands." At one stop Bates was accosted by a man demanding a miracle. "What shall I do for you?" Bates asked him. "Turn this cart wheel into a horse!" the man demanded. "That's just like the

evil one," Bates replied, "to leave the owner of the cart with only one wheel to go home with."

But for the most part the Kentucky revivalists welcomed the Shakers and the established practice that they offered. Hundreds, sometimes thousands, of people attended their meetings. In 1806 forty-four converts signed the covenant and established the first Shaker village in the West—Pleasant Hill, Kentucky. That same year two more villages were established in Ohio, and eventually three more would be built in the West, in Ohio, Kentucky, and Indiana.

We now had to go to work late and early to clear the lands and raise something for our support and build us a house to live in before the next winter set in. We built a log house weatherboarded it and lathed and plastered it which made quite a comfortable dwelling house. I would just observe that we pinned the shingles with lindel pins. We thought we was too poor to buy nails. Shaker journal, 1806

Although the land for Pleasant Hill was donated by a convert, like all the village sites, it was an ideal location. Atop a lush bluegrass hill, it was just a mile from the Kentucky River, a roadway of commerce in the wilderness. From the river's high palisades came the limestone for the buildings. "We thought it prudent to build with stone because we have a number of quarries of the best quality, and our timber is likely to be scarce." But the eastern Shakers were unfamiliar with the material, and their first limestone house, built in 1809, was not "perfect" according to their expectations. So in 1811, after studying with local craftsmen, they built a second

Ministry shop, Pleasant Hill.   Although elders and
eldresses worked as hard as ordinary Believers, they did
so separately. The ministry shop housed the leadership
upstairs and provided them with workshops downstairs.

1811 limestone shop, Pleasant Hill. The western Shakers used limestone for the first time when they began to build in Kentucky, and their original limestone building was not perfect according to their standards. So in 1811, the Shakers built another, identical building. This one was nearly flawless.

Opposite: 1809 limestone shop, Pleasant Hill.

limestone building of precisely the same design, and this time it was flawless.

The house is well finished off in all its parts, and is admired for its beauty and convenience both in worksmanship and plan. The work is done in a plain modist stile. As to the people that live in it, with regard to their faith and obedience, their faculties and zeal, we do not know but that they are equally beautiful as their house. Shaker journal, 1811

Eventually 266 buildings were constructed at Pleasant Hill to house five hundred people and dozens of industries. The buildings followed the codes set at New Lebanon, but Kentucky's climate and resources required certain practical modifications. These modifications turned into an architectural style as distinct from

the eastern villages as it was unique in Kentucky.

May 7, 1833. We have built a nice little frame building over our water cistern for the purpose of keeping the water cool in the summer and from freezing in the winter.

Shaker journal

The western Shakers were particularly inventive and progressive. Pleasant Hill was the first settlement in Kentucky to have running water, and only the second to have it west of the Alleghenies. The Shakers traveled the Kentucky, Ohio, and Mississippi rivers in flatboats trading their products, produce, and livestock as far away as New Orleans. And they insured their cargo. When a boat laden with $1,100 worth of Shaker goods burned at the

wharf in Louisville, the Shakers were quite satisfied that they were "paid in full without the trouble of taking them to Orleans." The western Shakers were the first to bind books, and they distilled whiskey for sale. For a time one society ran a hotel. And they were especially renowned for their wild-eyed strain of short-horn cattle. Shaker sisters raised silkworms and wove and wore fine silk. Though it was prized by merchants, Shakers made silk only for their own use. They did, however, sell it to the eastern societies, at a price, an eldress complained, "that might seem middling high."

Most progressive of all was their attitude toward slavery. By 1817 the Shakers unequivocally condemned it and refused admittance to converts unless they would sign a document freeing their slaves. Slaves who wished to join the Shakers with their masters were admitted as equal members of the family and were fully integrated into every aspect of life. The Shakers even went so far as to buy slaves in order to set them free.

Today we purchased Jonas Crutcher, a colored man who has been a Believer about 19 years. We have bought him to prevent his being sold south. He was accepted on equal terms.

Shaker journal

By 1825 there were eighteen hundred Believers in seven villages in the West. The villages were as beautiful and prosperous, as productive and well respected as their counterparts in the East. And every cent of money that was spent by the eastern societies toward establishing the western villages was repaid in full. Still, Indiana was the farthest west the Shakers got. The frontier moved on without them.

Meetinghouse, Pleasant Hill.   Twin entrances were
provided in every building—one for men and one for women,
so that they need never cross paths. Inside, polarity
was maintained with separate doors and stairways.

Center family dwelling, Pleasant Hill.

Meetingroom, center family dwelling,
Pleasant Hill.

Spiral staircase, trustee's house, Pleasant Hill. The three-story, twin-spiral staircases are considered by many to be the pinnacle of Shaker architecture. They were designed to conserve space by Brother Micajah Burnett, who is credited with the architectural distinctiveness of the village. In addition to his architectural designs, Brother Micajah was "an accomplished civil engineer, a master mathematician, a competent surveyor, a mechanic and machinist of the first order and a good millwright, and withall, a firmly established, honest-hearted Christian Shaker."

THE TWELVE VIRTUES

FAITH   Divine faith is that pure influence proceeding from the eternal source of all good, which plants the seed of God in the soul

HOPE   Tho' souls may receive the true faith of the gospel; yet without hope no one would be able to set out in the cross-bearing work which faith unfolds

HONESTY   The virtue of honesty is the operation of the righteousness in man, and plants the principle of uprightness in the soul

CONTINENCE   It is the principle of self-denial and abstinence from all evil; the source of seclusion or separation from the principles and practices of the world and the spring from whence proceeds the virgin life

INNOCENCE   The operation of continence destroys all fleshly lust, and implants in the soul the virtue of innocence

SIMPLICITY   Implies a Godly sincerity, and real singleness of heart, in all our conversation and conduct. This virtue is the operation of holiness and goodness and produces in the soul a perfect oneness of character in all things

MEEKNESS   This is that mild, gentle and unassuming virtue which is the very opposite of pride and haughtiness. Meekness readily leads the soul to obedience to God

HUMILITY   That principle of virtue, exercised in modesty, which produces a wise, sober, cautious, discreet and amiable deportment in conduct and conversation

PRUDENCE   Leads to a discreet, judicious and wise improvement of every natural and moral faculty, and of all the powers, gifts and graces given of God to man. Temperance is one of the distinguishing graces of prudence

PATIENCE   It enables the soul to bear up under the severest trials and to persevere through the greatest difficulties. It is always subject to the will of God

THANKFULNESS   A soul in the possession of the genuine love of God feels a sense of his unbounded goodness; and is thereby feelingly excited to a holy fervor of heavenly joy and gratitude

CHARITY   It is that benevolent principle which kindly administers whatever is truly needful for the benefit, support and happiness of soul and body, each in its proper order. It administers indeed the treasures brought forth by all the other virtues

THE WORLD'S PEOPLE

The Shakers are a celibate order, composed of men and women living together in what they call "families" and having agriculture as the base of their industry. They have a uniform style of dress; call each other by their first names, say yea and nay, but not thee and thou. In practical life they are industrious, peaceful, honest, highly ingenious, patient of toil and extraordinarily clean.

Charles Nordhoff, 1875

The women, old and young, ugly and pretty, dress in the same neat but un-fashionable attire. There are no bright colors; no ruffles or flounces or frills; no embroidery or laces; no ribbons or ornaments of any kind. The hair is combed back smoothly under a plain cap; a three-cornered kerchief of sober brown covers the bosom, and the narrow gored skirt has no room for crinoline.

Thomas Lowe Nichols, 1864

In appearance they are often simple; but they are men with ideas, men capable of sacrifice. Unlike the mass of mankind, who live to make money, the Shakers soar above the level of all common vices and temptations, and from the height of their unselfish virtue, offer to the worn and wearied spirit a gift of peace and a place of rest.

Hepworth Dixon, 1867

They are noted for cleanliness, industry, honesty, regularity and benevolence, but they are especially held up to censure and ridicule because they dance to the honor of God.

Friderich von Raumer, 1846

Left: Meetinghouse, Sabbathday Lake. Built high into either side of the meetingroom were small, louvered windows where one brother and one sister, assigned to be "monitors," would observe the service and note "irregularities of conduct."

Right: Elder Daniel Sizer with newspaper. Between the years 1871 and 1900, the Shakers published their own newspaper, printed at Canterbury under various names including *The.Shaker, Shaker and Shakeress,* and *The Manifesto.* The paper included home notes from the villages, obituaries, book reviews, and advice on being a good Shaker.

Stairway to fifth floor attic,
dwelling, Hancock.

4. HEARTS TO GOD

I never did believe
That I ever could be saved
Without giving up all to God.
So I freely give my whole,
My body and my soul,
To the Lord God, Amen
            Shaker hymn

I arrived at their town on Sunday, around 11
o'clock. When I got in view of their church, I
heard a doleful noise. As I approached nearer,
the sound broke with increasing strength on my
ears, the air was filled with piercing shrieks,
shouts, and confused acclamations resembling
the wild and maddened tenants of bedlam. I
was told that the Shakers were at worship.
        Richmond Inquirer, Massachusetts, 1825

On Sundays the Shakers danced to the honor of God. Their worship was an exuberant spectacle that veered unpredictably through many hours of the day. Formal dances could at any time break off into spontaneous displays of whirling, weeping, and shaking. Scathing or uplifting sermons were delivered extemporaneously by the elders, or by individual worshipers who were suddenly seized by the power of God and compelled to speak. Thousands of spectators packed the little meetinghouses to be entertained, shocked, or inspired. No one who witnessed Shaker worship, whether horrified or enraptured, ever forgot it.

Entered with a flock of other "females" the female door, got a good seat in the middle of the side appropriated for "world's people" and awaited the performances as at a theatre. Very gradually, Shakeress after Shakeress opened noiselessly their side door, glided on tiptoe noiselessly across the beautiful floor to their respective pegs, hung thereon their white shawls and straw bonnets, then sat down, as jointed dolls do, upon the wall benches, handkerchief straight across lap and hands folded over, turning not an eyelash to the right or left, like so many draped sphinxes or corpses set on end. After utter repose the men and women staring at each other from their respective benches, rather dangerously if eyes are ammunition to such sanctified shadows of humanity, they all rose, or rather stiffened up their joints like a machine, and putting back the benches began to sing, one of the elders addressing them in unconnected, drawling scraps of morality, pitying us for our poor, lost condition, declaring them the favored of Heaven, and prophesying that one day we should lament we were not Shakers! They then filed off in a double circle, one circle going one way, another, two or three abreast, "laboring" round this large hall, knees bent, with a sort of galvanized hop, hands paddling like fins and voices chanting wild airs like so many old witches working over the cauldron. But no witches sabbath, no bacchanal procession could be more unearthly, revolting, oppressive, and bewildering. The machinery of their stereotyped steps, plunging on in this way so long without rest, the constrained attitude forward, the spasmodic jumps and twists of the neck, and the ghastly visages of the women in their corpse-like caps, the waving of so many shrill voices, and the rigid expression of their faces combined to form a spectacle as piteous as disgusting, fit only for the dancing hall of the lower regions or the creation of a nightmare.   Fanny Appleton Longfellow

"Congregation of strangers after leaving church, Jn 30, 1878," Canterbury.
Sunday worship at the Shaker villages was open to the public for many decades, and 500–600 visitors sometimes packed the tiny meetinghouses. The Shakers referred to all non-Shakers as "world's people."

Whirling dance, lithograph.   "We hear of people
crucifying their sinful afflictions everywhere,
yet it is here alone that we are permitted
to observe the process."   *Horace Greeley*

Women and children dancing, lithograph. Shaker dancing was the subject of wild rumors and speculation. For those outsiders who could not attend services themselves, lithographs, which were often quite distorted, became very popular.

As I gazed upon the congregation of four or five hundred worshippers marching and countermarching in perfect time, I felt certain that were it seen upon a stage as a theatrical exhibition, the involuntary exclamation of even the hypercritical would be "How beautiful!" The women, clad in white and moving gracefully, appeared ethereal, and among them were a few very beautiful faces. All appeared happy, and upon each face rested the light of dignified serenity. Benson Lossing, 1857

Their faces were enraptured, they rose and rose in their march with a glad exultation. It was a thrilling sight. To the worshippers, this part of their rite was evidently that sort of joy which, if physical, is next to spiritual transport. William Dean Howells, 1876

For the Shakers, their unconventional worship was the fire in which worldliness, greed, and carnality were burned away and where pure contact with God and with each other was forged. The combination of "deep mental and religious fervor" with rhythmic body motions created within the Believer "great spiritual inspiration." "I have seen," an elderly Shaker reported, "the perfect spiritual union that was produced when a soul combined the physical motions, the singing voice and the dedicated heart in giving praise and thanks to God."

There is evidently no labor which so fully absorbs all the faculties of soul and body as real spiritual devotion and energetic exercise in sacred worship. Therefore there is no operation that has so much effect to mortify and weaken the power of the flesh and energize the soul with the life of the heavenly spirit. It is an enjoyment far superior to any natural recreation or carnal pleasure—in no earthly pursuit whatever have I experienced such delightful feelings or such as would bear any real comparison to what I have felt in sacred devotion. Elder Calvin Green, 1823

April, 1827. Sabbath
Each one sung what he felt the most gift in, and every song was full of love; David seemed to be devoted to helping the youth, for every time I saw him he had hold of some one of them by the hand and was leading them on to God; Isaac Youngs had little James in his arms with his little hands clinched fast around his neck, marching round. He said he felt very unwell and hardly able to come to meeting when he came, but now he felt like another creature. Sister Elizabeth Lovegrove

The form of Shaker worship was brought from England by Mother Ann, where she had learned the frantic dancing that gave the sect its name. The Shaking Quakers welcomed the "supernatural effects of the power of God" as they were transformed into "instruments" of the spirit world, dancing uncontrollably and speaking in unknown tongues. This religious frenzy was not unique to the Wardleys, nor was it unique in America. It was a common manifestation of charismatic religions, and Mother Ann found it quite familiar to rural revivalists. With the for-

"Warring song"

"Quick march"

"Humility"

malization of Shakerism after Mother Ann's death, spontaneous shaking was transformed into ritualized, rehearsed dances with complicated steps and patterns. Although individuals were still free to speak or sing or dance, it was usually done in a more orderly manner. But the unifying spiritual effect remained the same, and totally spontaneous expression never ceased entirely.

The music was unlike anything I had ever heard; beautiful, impressive, and deeply solemn. Their songs and hymns breathe a pure and Christian spirit; and their music captivates the ear because of its severe simplicity and perfect melody. Benson Lossing

Sometimes the hands are raised, palms outward, and the position shifted with such velocity as to indicate the lively, sweet and beautiful motions of the heavenly spirits, untainted with the flesh. They sing in the gift of the spirit the most beautiful songs and words. They appear like beautiful spirits moving in their appropriate element—Mother's pure love, carried in the power of God, unbodied spirits rather than inhabitants of this earth.

Brother John Dunlavy

Song was always a fundamental part of Shaker worship. In simple rhymes Shakers were able to convey to each other complex ideas and understandings, and the beautiful, uncluttered melodies added an emotional current that gave the words additional force. "Songs have so many messages in them," Sister Mildred Barker says, "and very often if you can't express it yourself, the words to the songs bring it out. I have found so many answers to so many things in the songs."

More than ten thousand Shaker songs were written down, many of them particularly treasured because they were "gifts of the spirit," "received" by Believers through inspiration rather than written and composed. A sister at New Lebanon was known for receiving songs in her sleep, which her roommates wrote down as she sang them because she herself never remembered in the morning.

The Shakers also had a unique system for notating songs, using the letters of the alphabet rather than the notes on a scale. The author of the system claimed that it was imparted by inspiration from Mother Ann.

The poetry is hardly up to our literary standards, but the music has always been something sweet, wild and naive.

William Dean Howells

"Giving and receiving brotherly love."

Shaker sisters demonstrating dance positions.
"God has created nothing in vain. He created the hands and feet.
Shall these important faculties be active in the service
of sin, and yet be idle in the service of God?"

I will bow and be simple, *I will bow this is the token,*
I will bow and be free, *I will wear the easy yoke,*
I will bow and be humble, *I will bow and be broken,*
Yea bow like the willow tree. *Yea I'll fall upon the rock.*

Shaker hymn

The world's people would attend their religious services on Sunday evenings and watch them go round and round in their dance, and think them the most impractical visionaries on earth. The next morning at sunrise, these same neighbors who had business at the mill would find the Shakers hard at work warping logs to the saw frame, and their conversation and deportment were as grave and serious as their religious exercises had been inexplicable the night before. Sister Mildred Barker, 1967

Shakerism was a daily practice. Sunday worship was not meant to satisfy religious aspirations, so that they might be comfortably forgotten during a week that had other priorities. On Monday morning Believers began a week of religious activity in perfect contrast to the exuberant disorder of Sunday worship, but with precisely the same aim. During the week inspiration gave way to order, and hard work and rigid discipline became the foundation of their practice. The essential religious tenets of Shakerism were enacted through a routine of minutely prescribed rituals designed to put Believers in relation to their spiritual aims *all day*, through every gesture, while pursuing the ordinary functions of life. The practicing Shaker was held accountable to his religion when he stepped out of bed, when he dressed, when he ate, when he spoke, and when he worked. The worldly lusts that were exorcized on Sunday were now suppressed

Round barn, Hancock.
"January 13, 1844. Some rainy
in the morning, and some splashy.
Elijah Myrick makes alot of broom handles."

Opposite, top: Washhouse, Hancock.

Opposite, bottom: Mount Lebanon. "The beautiful, as you call it, is absurd and abnormal. It has no business with us." *Elder Frederick Evans*

by rules: carnality was held at bay by a dress code that insured modesty, by a series of orders restricting the body's movements and appetites, and by architectural designs that segregated the sexes. Unity was enforced by the requirement of obedience—the submission of the individual will to the authority of God's appointed leaders. During the week the Shakers believed that by keeping their inner and outer lives in perfect order they were reflecting the perfect order of God's kingdom. "Order is heaven's first law," an elder wrote. "Without order, there is no God."

Not a single action in life, whether spiritual or temporal, from the first initiative of confession to that of dressing the right side first, stepping first with the right foot as you ascend a flight of stairs, folding the hands with the right thumb and fingers above those of the left, kneeling and rising again with the right leg first, and harnessing first the right-hand beast, but that has a rule for its strict and perfect performance. Hervey Elkins, 1853

The Shakers claimed that this restraint was their liberation. They believed that in putting down the body the spirit was uplifted, that in submitting their will they lived by God's will, that by controlling the beast they freed the angel and earned the blessings of Heaven. Their daily ritual, they felt, was filled with deeper satisfactions than all the indulgences and freedoms the world provided to its people.

The Shaker is the freest soul on earth, because all of his bonds are self-imposed.
Elder Harvey Eads

Do not think they always wear somber faces. I have heard them roar with laughter, and have engaged them in the most lively conversation. They are of the same flesh and blood as other

people, only their discipline is of a different stamp. J. P. McLean, 1907

The daily ritual began at the first light of dawn with the sound of a bell at 4:30 A.M. in summer and 5:30 in winter. In fifteen minutes Believers washed and dressed, stripped their beds, knelt for a moment of silent prayer, and left the rooms for an hour of morning chores. The sisters moved through the dwelling, making beds and putting the rooms in order. Brethren milked the cows and fed the animals, started fires in the workshops, and completed preparations for the day's work.

Of course the brethren would get a whole day's work done before breakfast, so they were ready for a nice good breakfast—pie, apple pie in the morning always, because they were really hungry. Eldress Gertrude Soule, 1982

Shaker meals were taken in silence at long tables in a large dining room, the men seated on one side of the room and the women on the other. At the sound of a horn, brothers and sisters "marched" in through separate doorways, carefully graded from oldest to youngest. They knelt in silent prayer and then sat on long benches at the table. Platters of food were set at every four places to prevent reaching, and were replenished by the kitchen sisters as soon as they were emptied.

All should leave their work when the signal is given for them to gather in at meal time, and be in their rooms in readiness to repair to the dining room, in order and in the fear of God, keeping step together.

When you take a piece of bread, take a whole piece and when you cut meat, cut it square and equal, fat and lean, and take an equal portion of bones. Take it on your plate together with the sauce and not be cutting small pieces in the platter and putting them directly in your mouth.

If you are obliged to sneeze or cough, don't bespatter the victuals. Make use of your hand-kerchief.

It is not allowable to eat wheat bread the same day it is baked; for it is considered very un-wholesome.

When you have done eating, clean your plate, knife and fork—lay up your bones in a snug heap by the side of your plate—scrape up your crumbs—cross your knife and fork on your plate with the edge towards you.

And lastly, when you drink, never extend your under lip so far down that one would think the cup was agoing to be swallowed whole.

Table monitor

Opposite: Kitchen, center family dwelling, Pleasant Hill.

Left: Dining Room, family dwelling, Pleasant Hill. "Never put on silver spoons for me, nor tablecloths, but let your tables be clean enough to eat on without cloths; and if you do not know what to do with them, give them to the poor."*Mother Ann*

Above: Dining room, Mount Lebanon. Menu for supper, one evening in 1824: "Rye Indian bread, mutton, Irish potatoes, corn, apple pie, cranberry tarts and turnovers, pound cake, white bread."

Visible order was apparent everywhere in a Shaker community. Villages were laid out square, paths ran at right angles, and diagonal shortcuts were forbidden. Buildings were color coded according to their use: barns and service buildings were deep red or brown, workshops were yellow or cream, and the meetinghouse was the only building painted white. Within the buildings every room, every cupboard, every shelf was numbered so that even a spool of thread could be returned to its proper place.

One rocking chair is admissible in each room, but such a luxury is unencouraged; two lamps, one candlestand, bedsteads painted green, coverlets of a mixed color, blue and white, two or three bibles and all the religious works by the society. No image or portrait of anything upon the earth, or under the earth, consequently clocks and such articles purchased of the world go through the process of having all their superficial decorations erased from their surfaces.
Hervey Elkins

There were orders regulating rising and retiring, locks and keys, dooryards and farms, prudence, neatness, economy, and the dead. Relations between the sexes were regulated down to the proscription against sisters sewing buttons on the brethren's clothing while they were being worn. Men and women were forbidden to pass on the stairs, to shake hands, to speak alone together, or to hang their clothes side by side. Believers were not allowed to write with red ink, to mark their names on anything, or to lean on the outside of their shoes. Curtains must not flap out of

Top: Shoe forms, Pleasant Hill.   Up to the Civil War the Shakers made all their own clothes, including their shoes.
Bottom: Meetingroom, center family dwelling, Pleasant Hill.

Hancock.   Buildings at many villages were color coded
according to their use—barns and service buildings
were deep red or brown, workshops were yellow or
cream, and the meetinghouse was always white.

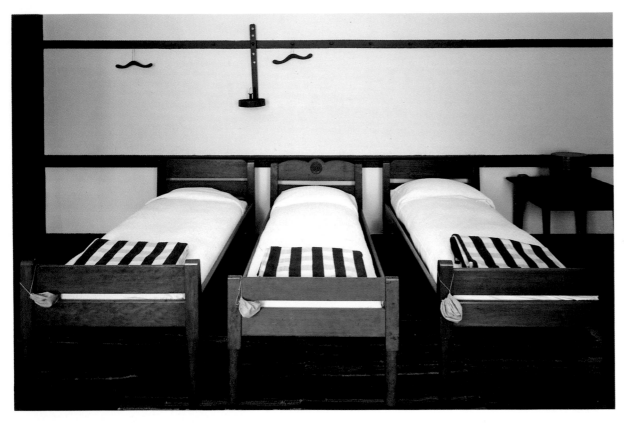

open windows. Doors and gates had to be shut, or fastened open to prevent swinging. "Vulgar expressions" such as "I wish I was dead!" or "My stars!" were strictly forbidden. At the end of the day Believers were told to "rest in the fear of God and lie straight."

Religious rituals continued well into the evening. At 8 P.M. a bell called everyone to "retire."

To retire is for the inmates of every room—generally from four to eight individuals—to dispose themselves in either one or two ranks and sit erect, with their hands folded upon their laps, and in that position labor for a true sense of their priviledge in the Zion of God—of the fact that God has prescribed a law which humbles and keeps them in the hollow of His hand, and has favored them with the blessing of worshipping Him. If any chance to fall asleep while thus mentally employed, they may rise and bow four times, or gently shake and resume their seats. Hervey Elkins

After half an hour another small bell called all Believers to evening meeting. Three nights a week were set apart for worship, one night there was no meeting so Believers could go to bed early, and three nights were reserved for "union meeting." Union meetings began in 1793 and were designed to satisfy the need for some kind of "correspondence" between

Top: Bedroom, center family dwelling, Pleasant Hill. Each bedroom was shared by three to seven men or women. Regulations strictly governed what items were allowed in each room, and anything ornamental was forbidden.

Bottom: Bedroom arranged for a union meeting, dwelling, Hancock. One evening each week, Believers attended "union meeting," in which six to eight men and women faced each other across a broad aisle to converse socially. "If they had not a spiritual union, they would have a carnal," Father Joseph had explained.

the sexes. "If they had not a spiritual union, they would have a carnal," Father Joseph had explained.

Union meetings were held in the brethren's bedrooms, where the brethren would be joined by an equal number of sisters. Two rows of chairs were set facing each other across an aisle five feet wide, and for an hour men and women would "converse simply, often facetiously, but rarely profoundly."

In fact, to say "agreeable things about nothing" is as common here as elsewhere. And what dignity or meaning could be said? Where talking of sacred subjects is not allowed under the pretext that it scatters those blessings which should be carefully treasured up; and bestowing much information concerning secular plans practiced by your own to the opposite sex is not approved; and where talk of literary matters would be termed pedantry and small display, nevertheless an hour passes away very agreeably. Hervey Elkins

The rigid daily order was directed and overseen by a pair of elders and eldresses, who were in turn directed by the central ministry at New Lebanon. They were the guides to whom perfect submission was required, and through whom spiritual growth was nurtured. They had the delicate and difficult job of rising to lead, never forgetting that they were still equal to those they led, and lowly in the eyes of God. They were required to strive to understand what was needed below them, by each individual and the society as a whole, and to understand what was intended above them, by the voice of God.

The Ministry and Elders are not considered infallible oracles, but the most appropriate for the time, occasion and locality. The Order is the *infallible institution, and where Ministry and Elders are governed by the Christ spirit, which constitutes that order, they are oracles of God. The administration is not that of man or woman in their human capacity, but Godliness acting through man and woman.*
Eldress Anna White, 1904

Humility was the key qualification. In order to be effective, leaders had to be strong and firm in their guidance, without growing personally prideful. "It is the gift and order of God that is to be respected, and not the person." Potential leaders were tested again and again for this quality.

It is common for the leaders to crowd down by humiliation, those whom they intend to ultimately promote to an official station, that such may learn how it feels to be slighted and humiliated, that they also not be deceived by the phantom of self-wisdom. Thus while holding one in contemplation for an office of trust and care, they first prove him—the cause unknown to himself—to see how much he can bear without exploding by impatience or faltering under trial. Hervey Elkins

It is the solemn and sacred requirement of God, that every member should keep the door open to his or her elders, by a free and honest confession of every ignorant and willful transgression of the holy and sacred orders or family in which they reside. And all are required to lay open to them, the true state and situation of their minds. Millennial Laws

Confession of sin before an elder—or witness of "God"—was an essential practice in Shakerism. Confession was considered to be "the door of Hope to the soul," the means of thoroughly repenting to "pass on to greater salvations."

When you feel a conviction for anything, tho' it may appear small to you—go to your elders

Eldress Aurelia Mace, Sabbathday Lake.

Eldress Emma King, Canterbury.

Elder Alexander, Groveland, New York.

Elder Giles Avery, Mount Lebanon.

and there seek a privilege to confess it, for if you allow yourself to keep it, you will grow hardened and finally fall away from the way of God. Shaker manuscript

Unwillingness to submit to the authority of the elders implied an unwillingness to submit to the will of God. Believers who argued with the elders, or expressed too many opinions about how decisions were made, "make very little progress in the gospel." "Such ones," Lucy Wright had said, "are the very ones that need these orders which they so oppose. True Believers are able to see the necessity of Order, and it is their life and support, and none can travel without it."

If you give way to a spirit of jealousy, and suffer yourselves to judge your elders and feel against them on account of any cross or gift of mortification which they may have administered for your good; or if you harbor a spirit of unreconciliation and are watching for iniquity, injustice, partiality and the like, you will have a hard row of it. Lucy Wright

When I first came, I heard nothing of obedience as the only way of salvation. The word of God, you told me, was in my own heart, not in what the elders said. Your Gospel seems like a tunnel; the farther I travel in, the narrower it grows. Brother Thomas Brown, 1812

There were, from time to time, leaders with poor judgment, and Believers whose genuine faith compelled them to act against the counsel of their elders. Very occasionally a leader was removed by the Lead Ministry, but most frequently Believers, who, for whatever reason, could not obey, were forced to leave.

God works by a system of mediation of his own appointed order. However splendid the talents, or however great the gifts of any, they can never gain their own order in the House of God without acknowledging in their real feelings the true line of order before them.
Elder Calvin Green

Whoever wants to be the highest
Must first come down to be the lowest;
And then ascend to be the highest
By keeping down to be the lowest.
Shaker hymn

• • • • • •

Above all else, Shaker worship and Shaker order were aimed at the root of all sin, "the doleful works of the flesh." On Sunday, and all week long, the structure and form of the Shakers' lives was designed to sustain believers in their pursuit of the virgin life.

Because she that is married careth for the things of this world, how she may please her husband, and he that is married careth for the things of the world, how he may please his wife, but the unmarried woman careth for the things of the Lord, that she may be holy both in body and spirit, and he that is unmarried careth for the things that belong to the Lord, how he may please the Lord.
New Testament (Eldress Anna White)

Ann Lee began her ascent from nine years of spiritual torment with a revelation about the fall of mankind and the root of sin. Celibacy, she was told by a vision of Jesus, was the foundation of redemption. Her entire teaching, and the organized religion that grew out of it, were based in this revelation. To the Shakers it is the most fundamental and inextricable element of their devotion to God.

What is there in the universe that has so sensible, so quick and ravashing an operation as a corresponding desire of the flesh in the different sexes? As a gushing fountain is more

Deacon's desk, Pleasant Hill.   Leadership in a village
was comprised of elders and eldresses, who were responsible
for the spiritual welfare and guidance of the village;
trustees, who traded with the world; and deacons
and deaconesses, who managed business within the village

Four Shaker men.   "The brethren's hair shall not be left unnecessarily long before, nor behind. It shall be cut square across the forehead and thence in a line with the bottom of the ear."

Five Shaker women.   "The sisters are required to comb their hair clean and straight back from the forepart of the head, and fasten it in a knot upon the back part with a pin made for that purpose. And to wear a straight, plain muslin cap, which shall come so closely over the face as to conceal the hair entirely."

powerful than an oozing stream; so that desire of carnal enjoyment is far more powerful than any other passion in human nature. Surely then that must be the fountainhead, the governing power that shuts the eyes, stops the ears, and stupefies the sense to all other objects of time or eternity, and swallows up the whole man in its own particular enjoyment.   Testimonies

The Shakers upheld Mother Ann's mandate with a very simple rationale. Spirit and body are opposed, they maintained, and the nuclear family is in direct opposition to the holy family. They believed that the generative life, the life of husband and wife, father and mother, children and houses and land, "confines the love principle to a small circle of which self is the center." The pleasures of family life took up the place in the heart where God might otherwise reside. The Shakers recognized that it was a difficult choice, "a heavy cross," and that great sacrifice was required. They never advocated cel-

ibacy for the world at large. "We bless marriage," says Eldress Gertrude Soule, "but we answer to a higher call."

The joys of a celibate life are far greater than I can make you know. They are indescribable.   Elder Frederick Evans

The vital statistics of our order show that those who from youth and upward live a virgin life average a greater length of years.
        Elder Daniel Fraser, 1880

I so abhor, and from my soul detest that bad spirit which would rob youth of its innocent pleasures, pluck from maturity and age their pleasant adornments, and make existence but a narrow path towards the grave. In stiff-necked, solemn-visaged piety I recognise the worst among the enemies of heaven and earth, who turn the marriage feasts of this poor world, not into wine, but gall.   Charles Dickens, 1842

Their thoughts are full of the one subject of celibacy: with what effect may be easily imag-

ined. Their religious exercises are disgustingly full of it. It cannot be otherwise; for they have no other interesting subject of thought beyond their daily routine of business; no objects in life, no wants, no hopes, no novelty of experience whatever. Their life is all dull work and no play.   Harriet Martineau

Celibacy bewildered and offended the world's people, and it brought upon the Shakers more misunderstanding and ridicule than any other practice. Skeptics reduced the significance of celibacy to the ravings of a woman who lost four children in infancy. Others assumed that it was merely a disguise for sublimated sexuality or even secret promiscuity. But the Shakers were quick to point out that celibacy did not make them unique in the history of religion. Their practice, they reminded critics, connected them directly to the revered Apostolic Church of Christ, and to the most devout branches of nearly every traditional religion.

That there is an element of continence in the human soul which will yet be more fully developed is most evident. It has manifested itself more or less from the beginning of the race. It cropped out in the community of Essenes among the Jews, and indeed the Nazarites before them, the Theraputae of Egypt and the monastics of all Europe during the whole Christian era. It may be traced among the Brahmins and ascetics of the East and has flourished for unknown ages among the followers of the Grand Lama in Tibet. The support of the vestal virgins in the Roman temples shows the innate veneration of the human soul for the continent and virgin character as connected with religion.

Brother R.W. Pelham, 1874

We are celibates; monks and nuns without bolts and bars. Elder Frederick Evans

But there was a gap between the aspiration to a "pure and virgin life" and its daily practice into which critics could legitimately lodge their arguments. For those struggling to suppress their sexuality the lofty dream of spiritual purity often became simply guilt, judgment, and law enforcement.

In the course of daily life the sexes were so effectively segregated that although they shared the same dwelling, there was virtually no contact between them. Separation was enforced through peer pressure, a complete lack of privacy, and even surveillance. At union meetings where the sexes had sanctioned exchanges to acquaint themselves with one another, any "soft words and kind, concentrated looks" were instantly detected, and the seating arrangements were altered. Members who had knowledge or even suspicion of liaisons between a brother and a sister were required to report it to their elders "lest

they participate in the guilt." At Pleasant Hill, observers were posted in two watchtowers on the roof of the dwelling to prevent secret trysts.

Those who have been most among them have been compelled to believe that the Shakers are, generally speaking, sincere, both in belief and in the practice of abstinence from sexual coition. It is quite true that sometimes young Shakers in whom the tender passion is not entirely subdued, fall in love with each other, but these generally contrive to leave the sect and go to the "world" to get married and reside.

Mr. Macdonald

April 24, 1864. Illinois Green absconded from the West Family. What a spectacle! Nearly forty years old and starting out in the wide world hunting flesh! Shaker journal

The Shakers were frequently scathing and unforgiving of members who gave in to their earthly urges, and many of the transgressors themselves suffered intensely from the judgment of their peers and from their own consciences. In 1871 Brother Ira Lawson and Sister Eliza Van Valen ran away from Hancock and took a train to Albany to be married. In the middle of the ceremony, at a fashionable hotel, Lawson was overcome with remorse. "I was conscience stricken. I was terrified. I was speechless for a while. Right then and there in the parlor of that wonderful hotel I decided to go no further in the path of wickedness and sin to which I had been so unwisely led by the tempter. I knew the marriage could not be undone, but it could remain unconsummated, and I determined that it should be." The couple returned to Hancock and were readmitted. Brother Ira eventually became an elder, but Eliza finally left for good.

Sister Corinna Bishop.

Elder Ira Lawson.

Upstairs hallway, dwelling, Hancock.   "In this building there
are fifty-eight doors, which are passed and repassed more than two
thousand times a day, opened and shut either by those who have
some fear and care, with softness, or by those who have neither
fear nor care, with a bang like a little sharp clap of thunder."

Another young woman, Sister Ellina, fell in love with a brother in her village, but the two decided that their commitment to Shakerism was paramount, and they resisted their attraction. Their affection for each other remained obvious, however, and though they maintained their vow of celibacy Sister Ellina was ostracized by her peers with "recriminations, arraignments, admonitions and menaces." Disgraced, she reluctantly agreed to move to another village. "Grief ineffable, grief incommensurable, grief unconquerable entered then her breast," a friend reported, "and rankled and festered and corroded her bosom till the day of her death." She died shortly after resettling.

1854
June 8   Harvey Lyman left Hancock and went to Springfield.
June 10   Mary Ann White left Enfield and went to Thompsonville.
June 22   H. Lyman and Mary Ann White were tied together with the galling cords of wedlock.

Shaker journal

The Shakers were ridiculed for the folly of celibacy above all because it appeared to be a headlong dive into obscurity. How could a sect that refused to reproduce itself hope to sustain its membership?

The Shakers filled their ranks by converting adults and adopting children. Many converts brought large families with them, and their children were also raised to become Shakers. Orphans and abandoned children were also welcomed, and many of them signed the covenant at age twenty-one. Celibacy may have been a factor in the Shakers' decline as it became more and more out of step with the times in the late nineteenth and early twentieth

Upstairs hallway, center family dwelling, Pleasant Hill.   "The buildings were made capacious with a view to receive the world when they shall be converted to Shakerism."

centuries, but for a hundred years it probably increased membership rather than reduced it.

For many people in the eighteenth and nineteenth centuries celibacy was not a problem but a solution. Raised to believe in a link between sin and sexuality, children grew up in fear of damnation for their sinful thoughts and actions. The celibate life freed them from this conflict and anxiety. And for women celibacy offered an alternative to the domination of father and husband. By breaking the sexual connection between men and women the Shakers provided a rare chance for independence, for what they called freedom from "slavish subjection."

The woman is not only subjected to the pains and sorrows of childbirth, but even in her conception she becomes subject to the libidinous passions of her husband. This slavish subjection is often carried to such shocking extent that many females have suffered unnatural and premature death in consequence of the unseasonable and excessive indulgence of this passion in man.   Elder Calvin Green

I want to be clean and holy all over,
That Mother's rich blessing my spirit
*   may cover.*
I'll brush up my garments as clean as I can,
That Mother may own me her white
*   little lamb.*

Shaker hymn

Garden and washhouse,
Hancock.

5. HANDS TO WORK

Do all your work as if you had a thousand years to live,
and as you would if you knew you must die tomorrow.
Ann Lee

We believed we were debtors to God in relation to each other and to all men, to improve our time and talents in this life in that manner in which we might be most useful.

Shaker covenant, 1795

Therefore our labor is to do good, in our day and generation, to all men as far as we are able, by faithfulness and frugality in the works of our hands. Shaker memorial, 1816

Work was also worship with the Shakers, an act of piety. It was the core of their day, the activity through which all religious principles could be practiced. Work provided a specific, daily opportunity to serve God by caring for what they did. Daily manual labors were directly intended to redeem the earth. Everything that was done, whether the crafting of a chair or the sowing of a seed, was to be executed with attentive, diligent care. No rush, no wage, no inferior tools or raw materials distracted the Shaker. All labor was consecrated, and even the most menial tasks were willingly attended, as they were dignified in the service of God.

A man can show his religion as much in measuring onions as he can in singing glory hallelujah.

You have no menial service—none of your community think work is degrading, while in society at large, many men are ashamed of work, and of course, ashamed of men (and women) who work and make them ashamed of themselves. Now the Shakers have completely done away with that evil as it seems to me. That is one of their great merits, and it is a very great one. Rev. Theodore Parker

The incidental fruits of consecrated labor were enormous. Cooperation and peaceful relations among members were virtually insured by the mandate that all Believers work equally, without regard for class, rank or seniority. Health and longevity were the rule in Shaker villages, attributable, according to the Shakers, to good, hard work. Beautiful villages, plentiful resources, and enormous economic prosperity inevitably resulted from "faithfulness and frugality in the works of our hands."

There is nothing like work, temperately pursued, to drive away the blues, dissipate mists and melancholy, cleanse the humors of the body and clarify mental horizons.

Brother Alonzo Hollister

The Shakers were carpenters, printers, and beekeepers, bakers and merchants, chemists and architects. They carded and spun wool and cotton and hatcheled flax. On their Shaker-built looms they wove towels, carpets, and spreads, and fabric for their own clothing and bedding. They made pipes and pens and nails, buttons and buckles, brooms and mops and hoes. They tanned hides and fashioned shoes, mittens, bridles, saddles, and whips. They made bricks, cut stone, ran lumber mills, and built their villages from the foundations up. They sold wines and sauces and jellies, pickles and sausage, medicines and herbal remedies. And they were famous for their cloaks, oval boxes, and chairs.

What are goods worth, unless they are full of genuine religion? Shaker Manifesto, 1872

Every commune, to prosper, must be founded, so far as its industry goes, on agriculture. Only

Sisters making maple candy, Canterbury. This was a thriving industry at Canterbury where the community cultivated one thousand maple trees for their sugar.

the simple labors of a farming people can hold a community together. Elder Frederick Evans

Most of all, the Shakers were farmers. An English traveler once wrote that he could always tell when he had come upon Shaker property "from the excellent improvements. Their fields, orchards, fences, cattle, etc. afford every proof of it, and in their extensive gardens all useful plants may be found, but for weeds, one might seek in vain."

The garden, to the Shakers, was "an index of the owner's mind." "If you would have a lovely garden," one Shaker said, "you should live a lovely life." Shaker agriculture was a direct extension of Shaker life—the proof or refutation of their dedication to God.

You see the men who till these fields, who tend these gardens, who train these vines, who plant these apple trees, have been drawn into putting their love into the daily task; and you hear with no surprise that these toilers consider their labor on the soil as part of their ritual, looking upon the earth as a stained and degraded sphere which they have been called to redeem from corruption and restore to God. Hepworth Dixon

A tree has its wants and wishes, and a man should study them as a teacher watches a child, to see what he can do. If you love the plant, and take heed of what it likes, you will be repaid by it. Elder Frederick Evans

In agriculture, as in everything the Shakers did, their attention had a practical as well as a religious purpose. Care yielded better crops, and the annual harvest of their love of the soil was enormous. Kitchen gardens produced enough fresh vegetables to feed the whole village through the summer months and to fill the storerooms with canned goods for the winter. Orchards and nurseries yielded apples, pears, cherries, peaches, quinces, currants, plums, and berries for baking, canning, sauces, and trade as far as England. Hens provided eggs, and cows supplied milk to the Shaker creameries for cheese and butter. Saxon and merino sheep were raised for wool, and flax plants were cultivated to make linen. Shakers grew hay and barley, wheat, oats, rye, corn, and potatoes. A thousand maple trees in Canterbury, New Hampshire, supplied a thriving maple-sugar industry. As late as 1900 the Shakers were the largest land-holders in that state.

An account of the produce, beef, pork, butter and cheese raised this year, 1843, in the church at Harvard: 115 bushels of corn, 130 bushels of rye, 150 of oats, 800 of potatoes, 100 of turnips, 52 of wheat, 2800 pounds of cheese, 969 pounds of butter, 3850 pounds of beef, 3900 pounds of pork, and four loads of pumpkins. Shaker journal

Opposite: Elder Charles Greaves with tools, Mount Lebanon. Beards were optional but unusual until 1875, when they were finally outlawed in the interests of uniformity. "As nearly all clean shaven brethren feel decidedly opposed to wearing the beard by requirement, therefore it is not, at present, wise to introduce beard wearing, in any style, as the uniform custom among Shakers."

Top: North family garden, New Lebanon, New York. The Shakers treated their gardens with great care. They were, as one Shaker put it "an index of the owner's mind." At New Lebanon alone, over 50 acres were cultivated for a "physics garden" to supply the medicinal herb industry.

Bottom: Elder Henry Blinn with beehives, Canterbury. Elder Henry tended bees, among other professions, including publishing and dentistry. One hot day he noticed that certain bees sat by the entrance of the hive and fanned their wings, so he invented adjustable wind vents to ventilate the hives—air conditioning for bees.

Only flowers were forbidden. It was contrary to order to cultivate anything "useless."

The rose bushes were planted along the sides of the road which ran through our village and were greatly admired by the passersby, but it was strongly impressed upon us that a rose was useful, not ornamental. It was not intended to please us by its color or its odor, its mission was to be made into rose-water, and if we thought of it in any other way we were making an idol of it and thereby imperiling our souls. Sister Marcia Bullard, 1906

The Shakers do not toil severely. They are not in a haste to be rich, and they have found that for their support it is not necessary to make labor painful. Many hands make light work, and where all are interested alike, they hold that labor may be, and is, a pleasure.
Charles Nordhoff

It is impossible to convey any adequate idea of the diligent industry and perseverance of this people. Wherever we went we found them all activity and contentment. But they have every inducement to perseverance. They are all on an equal footing. Mr. Melish

Men and women worked equally hard, but in jobs that never overlapped. The sisters were responsible for traditional women's duties: housekeeping, cleaning, cooking and baking, laundry, light gardening, sewing, spinning, dyeing, and fancy work. "Here we find women just as able as men in all business affairs, and far more spiritual," Elder Frederick Evans once told a visitor, but he explained that if a woman wanted to do a man's job, such as blacksmithing, she would be denied, because "this would bring men and women into relations which we do not think wise." The rule was occasionally bent. In

Round barn, Hancock.

Opposite: Interior, round barn.   The round stone barn was designed for economy of labor.
One farmer could stand in the middle and feed a whole herd in a few steps. It was built into a hill,
with ground level doors on all three stories. The hay was loaded in at the top and pitched
down to the animals below. "The Shakers never saw any sense in fighting against gravity."

1814 a storm at New Lebanon caused a dam to break, and muddy water swept through the village, damaging roads and gardens and carrying away two buildings. The women were told to assist the men in the repairs.

They came forth leaving their spinning wheels for wheelbarrows, the needle for a shovel and their brooms for a hoe and rake; and encountering the huge mass of rubbish like a band of strong men, with the assistance of a few brethren, the stone, gravel, wood, timber, and slabs were removed so that before night came on our streets, lanes and yard appeared tolerably decent again. Eldress Anna White

In the freedom of the community is found opportunity for every form of ability, for every grade of genius. Each finds his own peculiar gifts needed and valued by the rest; and in the recognition of his worth, the communist finds a chance to work along the lines of his best endowments, feeling that the results are of value and prized by those about him.
Eldress Anna White

Converts frequently brought expertise in various trades with them, and although this was usually put to use for the community, all members were encouraged to broaden their skills. Jobs were usually rotated on a monthly basis so that members

Top: Sister Mary Hazzard weaving, Mount Lebanon. Poplar was considered a "useless" wood, because it split too easily for furniture and didn't even burn well in a fire. So the Shakers, in their loathing of waste, cut the wood into small strips and, on specially designed looms, wove it into material for bonnets and boxes.

Bottom: Ironing room, Mount Lebanon. Brothers and sisters worked equally hard but in jobs that rarely overlapped. The intention was to prevent contact between the sexes as much as possible. Here is a rare instance of a man at work in a sisters' shop.

Ironing room, Hancock.   Ironing rooms had a large stove in the middle to heat a dozen or more
heavy metal irons. The rooms operated with great efficiency, but the Shakers at Sabbathday Lake sought
to further economize their time. By pressing a piece of linen between two sheets of chemically treated
paper, they invented the first wrinkle-proof cloth. The fabric was water-resistant too.

Left: Drying racks, laundry, Canterbury.   These sliding racks held the laundry for the entire village. The laundry was hauled from the Shaker-invented washing machines on the first floor by a dumb waiter to the room above the boiler. Steam pipes from the boiler ran under the racks so that the clothes dried in one day, even during cold or rain.

Right: Laundry, Canterbury.

Ironing room, Hancock.

Blacksmith's shop, Hancock.

became versatile, rarely got bored with their work, harbored no envy toward each other, and had no opportunity to become personally prideful of the products of their labor. Elder Henry Blinn came to Canterbury at fourteen. He began by sawing staves for pails, worked briefly on the farm, and then worked in the blacksmith shop. Then he apprenticed to the man who ran the carding mill and the stove, tinware, and cut-nail industries, eventually becoming manager of the mill. For eight years he taught children, and then took up his own study of printing and bookbinding, dentistry, and beekeeping. He also took his turn as night watchman and always helped at harvest time. Another elder, Giles Avery, whose manual employment included carpentry, plastering, plumbing, joinery, digging foundations, sawing stone, repairing buildings, making wagons and dippers, building cisterns, and orcharding, said, "How similar to colonization in a new country communal association is, that members of a community should be willing to turn a hand in any needed direction in order to render their best service in building up and sustaining the cause."

Every improvement relieving human toil, or facilitating labor, gives time and opportunity for moral, mechanical, scientific and intellectual improvement and the cultivation of the finer

Top: Steam engine and horse carts. "It must not be surmised that communism keeps down all ambition or dwarfs the intellect. The Shakers have published quite a list of inventions by their membership."

Bottom: Brother Alonzo Hollister and his vacuum pan evaporator. This invention was used to distill herbs in a vacuum at very low temperatures, thereby preserving their medicinal qualities. It was this machine that inspired Gail Borden to invent evaporated milk.

Top: Medicine cabinet, Pleasant Hill. The Shakers were world renowned for their herbal medicines, which were grown, distilled, bottled, and labeled in their own shops.
Bottom: Herbs drying, Hancock.

and higher qualities of the human mind.
Brother Elisha Myrick, 1855

The Shakers were inventors. Their sense of economy and loathing of waste extended to their own time and labor, and therefore anything that simplified work or eased life was welcomed.

We are not so superstitious in our notions, nor set in our views that we cannot alter when we have become sensible that such change will effect us for the good. Progression is one of the prominent points of our religious faith, and we endeavor to make it manifest in things spiritual and temporal. Brother D. A. Buckingham

Throughout the dwellings and workshops simple gadgets facilitated work: a pea sheller, an apple peeler and corer, a dough-kneading machine, a cream separator, a miniature railway to carry milk to the milk cellar, cranes for lifting clothes from the boiler. Improvements in heating, lighting, and ventilation were constantly being upgraded. Windows were set into interior walls so that even a closet would have "borrowed light."

A mania has seemed to take hold of some of the brothers for inventing and being skillful mechanics, and they are successful. It is rumored that one of our members is now studying out a plan for a flying machine. If such is the case, you may expect a visit from him.
Shaker Manifesto

The Shakers invented a washing machine and a fire engine, an electrical machine "for medical purposes," "hair caps" for bald brethren, a hernia truss, an improved sundial, and a "tone-o-meter" for setting the pitch of Shaker songs. They invented machines for reeling silk, threshing, and planing; an "atmospheric steam-engine," a revolving oven and a stove-cover lifter, the common clothespin, an improved plow, an improved waterwheel, a chimney cap, and a piano that folded out into a bedroom suite. A vacuum-pan evaporator invented by Brother Alonzo Hollister for drying herbs so impressed a visitor named Gail Borden that he asked permission to experiment with it himself, and made a fortune in evaporated milk. And the invention of the circular saw is credited to a Shaker sister.

With a few exceptions, the Shakers never patented their inventions but shared them openly with the world, feeling that it would be wrong "for the people of God to take advantage of their fellow creatures by securing patent rights and speculating thereon, as the children of the world generally do."

The Shakers were the first in this country to introduce botanical medical practice, the first roots, herbs and vegetable extracts for medicinal purposes placed on the market having borne the Shaker stamp. Eldress Anna White

The Shakers pioneered the industry of herbal medicine. Over fifty acres of land were cultivated at New Lebanon alone for a "physics garden," where herbs, roots, and bark were grown to be dried, powdered, distilled, or condensed for medicinal preparations. The Shakers made ointments, tinctures, and lotions, pills, syrups, extracts, oils, and fragrant waters. At one time the Shakers produced most of the opium made in America. Products offered relief for everything from asthma to constipation. In 1871 fourteen thousand bot-

Herb drying room, Hancock.

tles of Norwood's Tincture of Veratum alone were put up, and another year nearly a million labels were cut for medicinal products. The recipes were printed on the packages.

Take extract blue flag, culver, stillingis, poke, butternut, dandelion, each 6½ lbs. ext. princess pine 5 lbs. ext. mandrake 4 lbs. ext. gentian 2 lbs. ext. colecynth 2 lbs. ext. black cohosh 10 lbs. aloes 9 lbs. pow'd capalcum 1 lb. pow'd sasafrass 10 lbs. borate of soda 15 lbs. spirits of sea salt 12 lbs. 30 gallons sugar house syrup, water to make 90 gallons. MIX.

Another significant development spawned by the love of invention and agriculture was the garden-seed industry. The Shakers originated the idea of selling seeds in paper packets, and they invented all the machinery to cut, fold, paste, and print the bags in their own shops. As early as 1800 Shaker garden seeds were a "prominent industry." In 1836 the Shakers offered seventy kinds of seeds, including melon, mustard, onion, parsley, parsnip, six types of bean, and five types of cabbage. Their seeds were always of the highest quality, were never mixed with non-Shaker seeds, and were guaranteed.

Hard-headed, shrewd, sensible and practical, he neither cheats nor means to be cheated, prefers to give more than the contract demands, glories in keeping the top, middle and bottom layer equally good in every basket and barrel of fruit or vegetables sent to market under his name. Eldress Anna White

By the mid-nineteenth century Shaker

Canned goods, Hancock. The Shakers were nearly self-sufficient in their food supply and canned much produce for the winter months as well as for sale to the outside world.

String beans, Pleasant Hill.

merchants were a familiar sight across eastern and central America. Some traveled to ports and cities with huge shipments of goods; others traveled in one-horse wagons to farms across the countryside, peddling small items and fresh produce.

When the Shaker who came to sell vegetables and fruits passed before our farm, I always bought something. He was never willing to take money from my hands. If I remarked that the price was too high, he replied "just as you please." Then I placed upon the table the sum which I thought sufficient. If the price was satisfactory, he took it; if not, he climbed into his wagon without saying a word.
Marquise de la Tour du Pin, 1795

Trade with the world was considered a treacherous job for the merchants who left the isolation of the Shaker village to go to the "great and wicked cities." Traders were carefully chosen, and carried with them strict regulations and dire warnings. No unnecessary conversation was allowed, nor "disputing or inquiring into things which will serve to draw your sense from the pure way of God." "No new fashions, in manufacture, clothing or wares of any kind," were to be purchased or even asked about. No one could, "for the sake of curiosity," visit prisons, churches, ships, museums, theaters, or shops. No man and woman could travel alone together, and two Shaker brothers "should not let an undercreature, whether human or inhuman, get between them if they can consistently help it." On returning to the village all merchants first had to speak with their elders and describe every detail of the trip, every exchange and conversation. Then they were required to join the rear of the ranks during worship

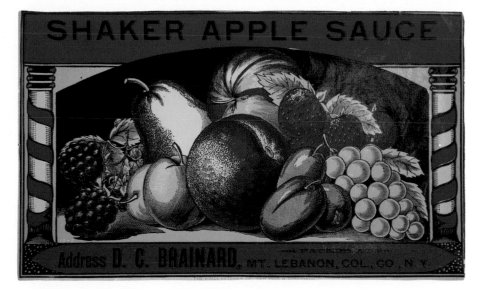

Seed label, *top*, and poster.
Although the Shakers shunned ornament in their own lives, they
accepted the practical considerations of good business and displayed a masterful
ability in the decorative arts when they advertised their goods to the world.

November 8, 1843. Smash and wash out the tomato seed.

October 14, 1845. Joel Turner, an old man almost seventy years old says he papers and pastes 400 bags in a day.

October 16, 1846. Pound out pepper seed. Squeeze and wash out the yellow tomatoe.

October 19, 1846. The sisters have put 35,000 papers of seeds for the western load.

October 21, 1846. Commence boxing for the western load. We gardeners alone box 15 nine dollar and 45 twelve dollar boxes.

October 26, 1846. We finish packing the western load of seeds. There is four, two-horse wagon loads.

January 9, 1847. Samuel W. says he has printed 30 thousand bags in one day when the press worked well and run steady.

January 25, 1847. Gideon had put up about 6000 papers of cucumber seeds this week.

February 3, 1847. Samuel W. has finished printing the common small bags; he has printed 200,000. Shaker journal.

until they had been back among Believers at least twenty-four hours.

Over all the United States, the seeds, plants, fruits, grain, cattle and manufactures furnished by any settlement of Shakers bears a premium in the market. There being no idleness among them, all are productive. There being no intemperance among them, none are destructive. There being no misers among them, nothing is hoarded or made to perish from want of use; so that while production and improvement are at their maximum, and waste and destruction are at their minimum, the society must go on increasing the extent and value of its temporal possessions, and thus increase its means of doing good, first within, and then beyond its own circle. J. S. Buckingham, 1838

Prosperity, the Shakers said, was an inadvertent product of consecrated labor. In the service of simplicity and perfection, they made things that were beautiful, durable, and highly valued in the marketplace. Shaker merchants were dependably honest, and people paid a premium for anything made in their workshops or grown in their fields. Shaker goods were frequently imitated but never successfully duplicated.

Is it strange that a celibate man, who puts his soul into the soil—who gives it all the affection which he would otherwise have lavished on wife and child—should excel a mere trading rival in the production of fruits and flowers?
Hepworth Dixon

It is well to have one's name such a synonym for honesty that anything called by it may be bought and sold with perfect confidence.
William Dean Howells

Garden shed, Hancock.

Prize ox and cart, Canterbury.
Far right: 1826 seed bill,
Tyringham, Massachusetts

May 17, 1842.   Fair and quite warm and pleasant. Fruit trees full in the blow. The prospect now is that we shall have a fruitful season.

March 23, 1842.   Thomas Holden and Alfred Collier are preparing to shingle the west side of the sheep barn. Augustus at getting butternut bark for coloring. Elijah Myrick at the mill sawing shingles. John Blanchard is at work here in the blacksmith shop at blacksmithing.

March 30, 1842.   Elder brother and Augustus are at work at the mill turning chair stuff, and sawing small sieve rims. The farmers are at work fixing fences.

Sept 18, 1842.   We commenced drying apples in the new dry house today. Samuel and boys are getting in corn and pumpkins. We do considerable at cutting apples this evening.

Sept 20, 1842.   Farmers digging stones in the long swamp. Samuel and boys digging potatoes and cutting stakes. Some of the brethren to work on the dry house and some at the rowen.

January 13, 1843.   Cloudy and some rainy. Thomas Holden and Elijah Myrick work at the mill last night. Elijah Myrick cut his thumb with a piece of glass very bad.

January 28, 1843.   An account of chairs made in this family in the year 1841 and 1842, Elder brother Thomas Hammond foreman in making chairs. Amount, including all sizes, 339. There was put at the office 83 common, 3 rocking chairs with arms, and six small ones—92 in all.

Feb. 17, 1843.   Clear. Continues very cold. Elijah Myrick finished the shingle machine today. Augustus went to the blacksmith's to get some work done. John Williams does some at planing posts. Brother John Chandler is cutting seed bags for this years.

April 24, 1843.   Augustus went to Harvard town to sell fruit trees.

April 25, 1843.   Augustus went to Littleton to sell peach trees.

April 26, 1843.   Augustus went to Lexington with fruit trees.

April 28, 1843.   We take up some over 500 fruit trees to sell.

July, 1843.   In the morning I commenced making clothespins for the great house. I turned pins all this week excepting Thursday I mended shoes. I turned 604 pins this week.

Seeds.

GARDEN SEEDS,
RAISED AT
TYRINGHAM,
Berkshire, County, Mass.
And put up in Papers, with the retailing Prices
of the SEEDS on them.

FOR SALE, By

Among which are the following :—

PAPERS.		Cents.	$	Cts.
2 Early Petersburg Peas,	-	8	-	16
3 Large White Marrowfat Pease,	-	8	-	24
3 Green Dwarf Marrowfat Pease	-	8	-	24
3 Strawberry Pease,	-	8	-	24
Early Bush Beans,	-	8		
10 Blood Beet,	-	8	-	40
6 Turnip Beet,	-	8	-	48
White Onion,	-	12		
6 Yellow Onion,	-	12	-	72
9 Red Onion,	-	12	-	1.04
4 Long White Turnip,	-	6	-	24
3 Orange Carrot,	-	6	-	18
16 Scarlet Radish,	-	6		96
2 Large Head Lettuce,	-	4	-	08
2 Green Head Lettuce,	-	4	-	08
White Lettuce,	-	4		
4 Early Lettuce,	-	4	-	32
4 Drum Head Winter Cabbage,	-	4	-	32
11 Early Cabbage,	-	4	-	44
4 Red Dutch Cabbage,	-	4	-	16
3 Dutch Bush Squash,	-	6	-	18
2 Crookneck Summer Squash,	-	6	-	12
Crookneck Winter Squash,	-	6		
13 Early Cucumber,	-	6	-	78
3 Long Cucumber,	-	6	-	18
1 Cluster Cucumber,	-	6	-	06

Canterbury.   The Shakers were renowned for intelligent
and economical farming practices. They were careful
to protect the land from erosion and periodically
planted a field with a "mulch crop" to be plowed
under where it could rot and replenish the soil.

6. REAPING THE HARVEST

No one can look into the heart of American society without seeing that these Shaker unions have a power upon men beyond that of mere numbers. Their influence on the course of American thought is out of all comparison with that of minor sects. A Shaker village is not only a new church, but a new nation.

Hepworth Dixon

August 5, 1843. It is a general time of health and prosperity in the different societies.

Shaker journal

Sixty years after Mother Ann's arrival in America seventeen Shaker communities were flourishing and nearly six thousand Believers lived in peaceful isolation, unimpeded by the world. Socially, economically, and spiritually, their foundations were firm. Membership was greater than ever. And in the eyes of the world they stood as powerful proof that social change was within the grasp of the striving spirit.

They present the sublime and hope inspiring spectacle of a community founded and built up on the conquest of the inexorable appetites: lust, avarice, ambition, revenge. They have solved for us the problem of the practicability of a social condition from which the twin curses, pauperism and servitude, shall be utterly banished. They have shown how pleasant may be the labors, how abundant the comforts of a community wherein no man aspires to be lord over his brethren, no man grasps for himself, but each is animated by a spirit of devotion to the common good. Horace Greeley, 1850

When you can see 17 communities of people whose every right is secured, whose every rational want is supplied, does it not demonstrate that all mankind may be made happy in this world? Our sisterhood are redeemed, the rights of women are theirs, the rights of property we enjoy. Capital and labor are at peace.

Elder Frederick Evans

In the 1840's social reform became a cause championed by hundreds of thousands of Americans. The Shakers had already enjoyed nearly a decade of respectful toleration by their neighbors, but now interest in and even veneration of their social system began to soar. Utopians from around the world held up the Shakers' example to inspire their own dreams. In a fever of idealism, hundreds of utopian experiments were launched across the country. It was the age of the Oneidans and the Perfectionists, the Rappites and the Harmonists, the Icarians, the Universalists, the Fourierists, the Zoarites, the Ephratans, and the Transcendentalists. Communitarians settled from Maine to Texas and Oregon.

We are all a little wild here with numerous projects of social reform. Not a reading man but has a draft of a new community in his waistcoat pocket. Ralph Waldo Emerson

Like the Shakers, some of these groups were strictly religious, and their original social designs were meant only to promote their religious life. Many other groups were purely nonsectarian, based on political or intellectual ideals or on dreams of a healthier, more equitable, more pleasure-filled, more prosperous life. The largest number by far were a mix of the two, loosely associating social justice with salvation, incorporating social innovations with vaguely prescribed religious practices. They tested a wide range of social forms with some type of communalism at their foundation. Many adopted unorthodox sexual practices as well. Several sects were celibate; the Mormons, notably, were polygamous; and the Oneidans practiced a polygamous "complex marriage."

Village scene, second family, New Lebanon.

Despite their differences, all these groups were bound by the common dream of a better life outside society. They did not advocate change from within the system, or by overthrowing it, but sought to create models of ideal societies from which universal reforms might eventually spread.

And nearly all of them admired the Shakers. Some even felt that the Shakers were the foundation on which the whole age of experimentation was based. Friederich Engels defended communism with the Shakers' example. Horace Greeley, editor of the New York *Tribune* and a proponent of Fourierism in America, found them inspirational. Robert Owen, the great English reformer, read of the Shakers and decided to locate his experiment in America. Charles Lane and Bronson Alcott, the inflexible Transcendentalists at Fruitlands, corresponded constantly with their neighbors, the Harvard and Shirley Shakers, and when their own experiment failed, Lane and his son joined the Shakers. John Humphrey Noyes, the father of Oneida, was said to bow to no man except Elder Frederick Evans of New Lebanon.

The example of the Shakers has demonstrated not merely that successful communism is subjectively possible, but that this nation is free enough to let it grow. It is no more than bare justice to say that we are indebted to the Shakers

Top: Group portrait, north family, Mount Lebanon. Elder Frederick Evans is seated in the center with a staff, and Eldress Anna White stands to his left with her hand on his chair.

Bottom: New Lebanon with second meetinghouse on the left. The construction of a meetinghouse was a sacred event, but the building itself was not. When this larger meetinghouse was built at New Lebanon in 1824, the original building (despite the fact that it was the very first Shaker building) became the warehouse for the garden seed industry.

94

Meetinghouse,
Sabbathday Lake.

*On the whole they lead a good and comfortable life, and if it were not for
their ridiculous religious ceremonies, a man could not do a wiser thing than to
join them. I spoke to them about becoming a member of their society,
but have come to no decision on that point*   Nathaniel Hawthorne, 1842

"The picnic." Shakers at leisure on a hilltop, Canaan, New York.

more than to any or all other social architects of modern times. Their success has been the solid capital that has upheld all the paper theories and counteracted the failures.

John Humphrey Noyes, 1870

The Shakers endured while most utopian communities, even those that borrowed most heavily from them, withered away. One of the most important factors in the Shakers' longevity was the rigor with which they separated serious applicants from the merely curious. The egalitarian principles of other utopian societies led them to admit all applicants, without discrimination. This almost always brought internal dissension and lack of common purpose among the membership. The Shakers, while open to anyone, made the path rather steep, so that applicants sorted themselves out. During this period of failing dreams, their policy was especially prudent.

In the Shakers I find one piece of belief in the doctrine that encourages them to open their door to any wayfaring man who proposes to come among them, for they say, the spirit will presently manifest to the man himself, and to the

society, whether he belongs among them. They do not receive him, and they do not reject him. And not in vain have they drudged in their fields and shuffled in their bruin dance if they have truly learned this much wisdom.

Ralph Waldo Emerson, 1860

Shaker applicants entered in slow stages. First they lived outside the village, in a novitiates' house or sometimes even with their own families. They retained their property while participating in all the daily activities at the village. "Too hasty surrender, in early enthusiasm is discouraged. Time, experience, knowledge of conditions without and the heart within are first required." After a probationary period lasting as long as two years, converts were finally allowed to consecrate their property and join the community. Shiftless or unworthy applicants invariably found Shaker life too demanding and drifted away on their own. The community was little affected by their having come and gone.

To a man or a woman not thoroughly and earnestly in love with an ascetic life, and deeply disgusted with the world, Shakerism would be unendurable. It is not a comfortable place for hypocrites or pretenders. Charles Nordhoff

The number of people professing interest in Shakerism commonly rose in the fall, especially in New England, where the winters are hard. They would come, one Shaker said, "with empty stomachs and empty trunks, and go off with both full as soon as the roses begin to bloom." These "winter Shakers," as they were known, were easily identified but were never turned away. In every applicant, the Shakers asserted, might be concealed "the germ of a true soul, an angel hidden in the block." Short of that, the Shakers believed that charity was a "heavenly gift of God" and should be practiced freely. "If ye have not this charity, ye are counted mean in the sight of God, and are as empty bubbles."

Charity was another institution that set the Shakers apart from other utopians. The tendency among communities was to maintain economic isolation, hoard what wealth they had, and guard their prosperity. In many cases prosperity became the catalyst of greed, dissension, and collapse. The Shakers, although living in intentional isolation from society, gave freely to the needy around them, "sufferers of fire, flood or famine," and even

Meetinghouse,
Sabbathday Lake.

shipped "clothing and provision" to Ireland during the potato famine, having read that "it was a time of much suffering there." At one time the Shakers in Canterbury noticed that some of their poorer neighbors were stealing vegetables from the gardens at night. In response, they planted extra crops.

We plant some for the Shakers, some for the thieves, and some for the crows. Thieves and crows have to eat too. Elder Arthur Bruce

Once Charles Tiffany, president of Tiffanys in New York, was visiting a resort near the Shaker village at Sabbathday Lake, Maine. He got lost walking in the woods and found himself, dusty and bedraggled, at the Shakers' door. Sister Aurelia Mace assumed he was a tramp, dusted him off, and fed him a good meal. Tiffany never told her who he was, but he sent the Shakers a silver tea service in gratitude.

I do think that if they could be prevailed upon to turn their settlement into a school to bring up young folk for the married state, they would be a blessing to the world, instead of a spectacle to show how much wisdom and how much folly may be mixed up together.
Catherine Sedgwick, 1824

The rearing of children was another key to the Shakers' social success. It earned the Shakers the gratitude and respect of their neighbors, swelled the ranks of their membership, and most important, satisfied the children's celibate caretakers. Children raised by the Shakers were notoriously healthier and better educated than their worldly counterparts, and

Schoolhouse, Canterbury.   The schoolhouse was a single story building until 1862, when a second story was added—beneath the old one. Rather than raise the roof, the Shakers jacked up the whole building and built four new walls at ground level.

Shaker villages became a repository for homeless or unwanted children. "Little children are nearer to the kingdom of heaven than those of riper age," Mother Ann taught. The Shakers found children "more easily instructed in the ways of God," and, like traditional parents, they placed their hopes for the future in the young.

You must take care of the rising generation; for if they are protected, the time will come when they will be the flower of the people of God.
Father James Whittaker

Shaker schools were so good that they were frequently attended by local children whose parents wanted a better education for them than was available at the world's schools. Girls as well as boys were instructed in geography, grammar, algebra, astronomy, and agricultural chemistry, as well as in the practical arts necessary to farm, keep house, and run the various industries. But while "literary" studies were considered important, religion was still primary, and too much education was considered "mere lumbar of the brain." Instruction in "self-governing" and the "principles of moral virtue" were the foundation of their education.

Though a man should gain all the natural knowledge in the universe, he should not thereby gain either the knowledge or power of salvation from sin. Elder Frederick Evans

By all accounts, children's amusements were as well tended as their education. They had picnics and sleigh rides and popcorn parties. Girls kept a flower garden, and boys went fishing.

Hiding beneath an arcade of the bridge, we would pull off our shoes and stockings and wade knee-deep in the water. Then, loading our

Top: Eldress Anna Case and girls husking corn. Children who entered a village with their parents were treated exactly as were orphans. Separated from their parents, they lived in the children's order and were raised by a Shaker caretaker. *Left:* Girl's gymnastics. *Right:* Shaker schoolhouse, Canterbury. The Shakers raised their children with great care. Academic education was exemplary, and spiritual, practical, and physical training were considered equally, if not more important. Local children were often sent by their parents to the Shaker schools, which were notoriously better than the public schools.

Group portrait, Hancock, 1891. One young boy and one elderly man are probably an accurate reflection of the balance of the sexes in the village during this period.

Despite charity and asceticism, the expectation of comforts and luxuries began to seep into Shaker villages, and dissatisfaction and longing for worldly things slowly grew. The world that had finally accepted the Shakers began to draw them away. Some found celibacy too difficult. Others simply could not sustain their faith. Hervey Elkins, who spent fifteen years with the Shakers at Enfield, New Hampshire, left because he wished for "an inexpressible something which was not there to be found." A few who left took the sacred rituals to the marketplace. A popular act at the Baltimore Circus was the performance of original dances by former members.

The rate of apostasies by children rose the most sharply. Eighty to ninety percent of Shaker children would leave the society by the age of twenty-one. "I never blamed them," says Eldress Gertrude Soule. "A child brought in as a little girl has no idea what the outside world is like, and she gets curious. I know. I'm curious too."

palm-leaf bonnets with dandelions, which looked like little white-capped Shakeresses, we would float them down the stream in a race, the boat which won being decorated with buttercups and violets.

Fifteen Years with the Shakers, 1872

August, 1851. J. D. took oldest boys to whiting pond fishing and for pleasure—We catched it by the ears! Shaker journal

. . . . . .

I do not see how it is possible, in the nature of things, for any true religion to continue long. For religion must necessarily produce industry and frugality, and this cannot but produce riches. But as riches increase, so will love of the world, in all its branches. John Wesley

By the 1840s the Shakers had become tremendously prosperous. Although they maintained their ascetic ways, the quantity and value of their carefully maintained land was enormous and their dwellings, mills, barns, and storehouses, their reputation as merchants, and their healthy and plentiful workforce had made the Shakers rich.

A concern for material gain is too often mingled, among the Shakers, with the loftiest thought, business occupies too large a place in their minds. In the customs of the primitive church, "and they lived together, they bought and sold and held all in common," the two traits, "they bought and sold" seem too greatly emphasized. Madame Thérèse Blanc

What in the name of reason does it mean that so many are going off nowadays? Is there none of the younger part that will abide and be good for something? Are we indeed unable to raise any children or youth among us?

Brother Isaac Youngs, 1837

August 20, 1829. E. Linch went after strawberries and did not return.

Shaker journal

Pleasant Hill Kentucky. This evening Polly Hoosier committed suicide by hanging herself. She committed the act in the sister's shop above the kitchen at the West family. Polly was 18 years of age, a large and likely woman and naturally agreeable and good, but she spoiled it all. Shaker journal, 1819

Dwelling, Canterbury.   Flowers were forbidden when the village
was established unless they had some useful application, but in later
years this restriction was relaxed. The bell on top of the
dwelling directed the whole village through the daily schedule.

Meetingroom,
dwelling, Hancock.

7. MOTHER ANN'S WORK

Divine inspiration is a voice that speaks from the spirit world to the soul of man. If he has any interest beyond this world, he should keep himself in a condition to hear that voice, understand its language, and bow to its requirements. Shaker pamphlet, 1856

By the end of the 1830s a whole generation of Shakers had grown up never having known Mother Ann. Time and prosperity had brought with them a certain laxity— worldly values and practices, carelessness and wastefulness, materialism and rebelliousness that alarmed the leadership. "Shakerism," an elder wrote, "had greatly fallen from that perfect order in which it was first established." The spark of Mother Ann's teachings, which had burned brightly after her death, seemed in danger of being extinguished by the weight of their successful form.

But on August 16, 1837, four girls in the Gathering Order at Watervliet went into a trance and began to whirl, as the first Shakers had during Mother Ann's lifetime. For several days they sang and talked about the angels. When their trance ended they explained that they had been taken on a visit to the spirit world. "They had heard some beautiful singing, had seen some pretty flowers, and had enjoyed a

lovely visit with companions of their own age." The news of the event hit the societies like a bolt of lightning and inaugurated a remarkable revival within Shakerism that lasted almost ten years. It was known as "Mother Ann's Work."

Oh what a change is now affected
Humiliation does abound
For great big I is now rejected
Do pray for me is the general sound.
        Sister Elizabeth Lovegrove

The Shakers had been spiritualists since Mother Ann's first "conversation" with the Christ spirit, but never before had communications been received by ordinary members or with such frequency, force, and directness. Rituals and daily routines were overturned, backsliders were thrown out, and the "operations" of the early years—trances, shaking, speaking in tongues—returned to their worship.

Many have become Shakers which in times past hardly deserved the name of Shaker at all! But now they shake wherever they go; whether at work or at table! And sometimes their shaking is so violent that it is nearly impossible to get any food into their mouths, and they have to leave the table without eating. It is truly a wonderful day. Numbers who have for years

been spiritually dead, have been raised to life, and are now living souls in the house of God. Lead Ministry, 1838

The spirits of Mother Ann and other departed Shakers, of George Washington and Christopher Columbus, Queen Esther and the Shawnee chief Tecumseh, spoke to the Shakers through mediums.

Meetings were electrifying as one by one worshipers were "suddenly seized by that mysterious power, apparently to compel them to yield and speak what was

Shaker women and girls.

Meetinghouse and dwelling, Canterbury.   Shaker
dwellings were designed to lock only from the inside.
"The circumstances of no one being outside the house at night
made it unnecessary to lock the door from without."

Shaker meeting, September 20, 1885, Sabbathday Lake. This is the only known photograph of a Shaker meeting.

given by the spirit." The solemn message was very clear. Believers had grown forgetful of the call to purity and simplicity. Spirit messages pinpointed the transgressions. Sisters gossiped and went to bed late, talked before kneeling in the morning, and combed their hair in the kitchen. Brethren prayed with their eyes open, left lamps lit and stove doors ajar at night. There was dirt in the kitchen and dining room, marks on the stair railings, and tools in the wrong cupboards. There was waste in the workshops, vanity in the dressing rooms, and levity at the table. Everywhere the spirits reported a "slack, careless, and extravagant sense and feeling with regard to temporal things."

The insincerity of individual transgressors was publicly exposed. At one meeting two young mediums from another village were brought to review the worshipers. "Throughout the assembly pallid faces, tears and trembling limbs were visible. Anxiety and excitement were felt in every mind as all believed the instruments sacredly and superhumanly inspired. They stopped before each one as though reading the condition of every heart. As they passed some, they evinced pleasure, as

they passed others, they bespoke grief; others yet an obvious contempt; by which it seemed they looked within and saw with delight or horror the state of all."

December, 1842. This month a gift was announced for everyone to make a review of his life. For three weeks it was almost a perpetual Sabbath. Temporal duties, except those that were absolutely necessary, were mostly laid aside. Meetings were held at all hours.

Shaker journal

On the evening on Monday, February 3rd, Mother Ann was announced as present in the meeting. The medium walked the floor under a pressure of the spirit and audibly wept, and at last broke forth in anguish while holding in remembrance the present and future of God's

people. The gift was accepted and flowed from soul to soul. Individuals were in every attitude of prayer. Tears and cries were the offerings that came from every class and age in the family. Shaker journal

The revival woke Shakerism up. No Believer went unaffected. Devoutness and asceticism were generally restored; "hypocrites" were ejected, and the "lukewarm" became hot.

I have prayed with all my heart to be a partaker in the present gift. Some may say, "I guess George is going to be religious now," and so I am, for the judgments of God will soon come upon us if we do not wake up and labor for the power of God—this is my determination.

Brother George Wollison

I can truly say the brethren and sisters in this place have entered into the present gift beyond, yea, far beyond what I could have expected. It truly appears like one of the great miracles to see and sense the change which has already been affected. Since those refreshing showers from heaven descended, the drooping spirits have revived and the withered plants spring up. And, as it were, the dry forest begins to bud and blossom, and to leap for joy.

Elder Grove Wright, 1837

Most Believers were ecstatic with the revitalization of their lives. Religious influence and inspiration once again pervaded daily life, and even the youngest members were swept up in the "miracle." Every day new songs, new revelations, new visions, new prophesies were "received" through mediums. Invisible "spiritual gifts" bearing the names of material things were distributed freely to believers: precious gems, bags of gold, spectacles to see spiritual things more clearly, guns from George Washington to kill "old ugly," and spiritual wine, which made the partakers appear drunk. Most of these represented precisely the material goods that the Shakers were denied in their lives. A medium speaking in the name of a spirit explained that they "must be used in a proper line of sensation, for they are all spiritual."

They have been sent forth in this degree of nearness and semblance to material things that do exist on earth, that you might be better able to appreciate in lively colors and thrilling sen-

Tree of Light, "seen and received" by sister Hannah Cohoon, October 9th, 1845. This is one of many dozen magnificent pieces of art called "spirit drawings" by the Shakers, which were "received" in visions and painted despite regulations against such ornament.

Bottom: Spirit drawing.

Spirit drawing.   "Here is an emblem of the world above, where saints in order are combined in love."
The "saints" depicted across the top row are Mother Ann, Father James, Father William, and
Christopher Columbus.

sations the real adornings and beauties of the spiritual world, of which this world and all the arts of man's inventions are but a dismal, gloomy, and imperfect figure.

Brother Philemon Stewart

Even those members who did not have direct contact with the spirits participated with conviction. A Shaker from Tyringham named Robert Wilcox described being sent to Watervliet to tour the orchards there. His guide was a well-known Shaker medium. When Brother Robert was ready to leave the medium handed him something that he described as a white pear, to be delivered to a sister at home who was also a medium. Brother Robert could not see the pear but claimed to be able to feel its weight in his pocket. When he got home the sister took the pear from his hand before he had a chance to explain what it was. "How kind of him to send me such a lovely white pear," she said.

I saw the whole tree as the angel held it before me, as distinctly as I ever saw a natural tree. I felt very cautious when I took hold of it, lest the blaze should touch my hand. Seen and received by Hannah Cohoon in the City of Peace, Sabbath, October 9th, 10th hour AM, 1845. Drawn and painted by the same hand.

The most enduring manifestations of Mother Ann's Work are the "spirit drawings," images that were received and painted by several young girls despite the orders against ornament and decoration. Birds and angels and paper hearts filled with verses expressing "Mother's love" were drawn and given as gifts between the sisters.

*This pretty gift I send to you
That you at times may sit and view
This emblem of a higher sphere,
And bring your feelings to it near.*

Group portrait of children outside dwelling, Hancock.

On Saturday night the 6th of July 1844, we were aroused with an unmistakable midnight cry. Four sisters accompanied by their elders passed through all the sleeping apartments of the sisters, singing a piece having the title midnight cry, which was received for the occasion. Two hours after this a company of brethren passed through all the sleeping apartments of the brethren, and as might be expected, the whole family were soon up, and at 3 o'clock had assembled for a morning meeting.

Spontaneous acts became new rituals that embellished the Shakers worship. The Midnight Cry was an annual event for the next eight years. The "Sweeping Gift" became another annual rite, in which a group of singers and elders led a band of mediums through the village, removing "evil spirits" with "spiritual brooms." An actual cleanup effort accompanied the Sweeping Gift, "so that even a Shaker village, so notorius for neatness, wore an aspect fifty percent more tidy than usual."

In 1842 each society was told to prepare a holy place of worship on a hill nearby, the exact spot to be pointed out by a me-

dium, where a biannual feast day would be held. Fasting and confessions preceded these feast days, and then all "purified souls" received elaborate imaginary costumes in bright colors with silver and gold trim, "emblematic of the virtues of holiness, innocence, meekness, freedom and peace." At the holy hill they danced and sang, and conversed with departed spirits ranging from Mother Ann to Napoleon. Sometimes whole tribes of deceased Indians came to teach new songs and dances. A spiritual feast ended the ritual.

Our spirits were refreshed with holy water, with the wine of the kingdom, with the fool-ishness which confounds the wisdom of the wise, with grapes from the kingdom, with plums, with pears, peaches, strawberries, cocoanuts, pineapples, oranges, lemons, maple sugar, white sugar and everything that hearts could desire. Sister Sally Bushnell, 1841

In the evening when they returned to the village, Believers were "so bountifully supplied with spiritual food, that all hunger for natural food was not felt or realized."

Sabbath, November 6, 1842. Meeting at 2 o'clock in the meetinghouse. Marched from the meetinghouse to the vineyard where we wor-

shipped in God's grandeur. We sang, we danced, we shouted. Shaker journal

Sabbath, December 13, 1842. We kill chickens for the market this AM. Some of the Indians spirits make themselves known and speak in meeting this evening. Shaker journal

Sabbath, April 23, 1843. We had a very good meeting. In meeting about 22 hours. Shaker journal

In this extraordinary time of the outpouring of the spirit of Christ and of Mother, it is all important that the Ministry keep their eyes open and their spirits bright, so as to be able to distinguish clearly between the genuine spirit of Mother and that which is counterfeit; for we are sensible that young and inexperienced souls (as some of our visionists are) are liable to be inspired by an evil spirit, and think it Mother or some good spirit. Lead Ministry

By 1845 "gifts" were so frequent and commonplace that the course of the revival had become uncontrollable, and its force began to unwind. Lucy Wright had once warned Believers about the dangerous point at which "there could not a leaf move without its being a sign." Now individual mediums, who were often the youngest members, could claim to guide the whole family in the name of a spirit. Union among Believers and the authority of the leadership were both threatened. The Ministry began to require that all songs and messages be delivered directly to them, so that they could determine which were genuine and useful. One elder said that as the Devil had failed so far in

Top: Meetinghouse, Sabbathday Lake.

Meetinghouse, Hancock. Although a Moses Johnson meetinghouse was built at Hancock, it is no longer standing. This meetinghouse was moved to the village from the community at Shirley.

Canterbury.
"Every force has its form."

his plan to "destroy the union of God's people, his next stratagem was to effect it thro' inspiration."

I once swallowed down without doubting, everything that came in the shape of a message from the heavens, but after a while I got confounded by receiving a message in the name of Mother Ann, which I knew was a positive lie. From that time I found it necessary to be more on my guard. Elder Freegift Wells, 1850

The spirit manifestations also began to deteriorate, bringing pandemonium instead of inspiration. The Shakers explained that dead apostates and "vile spirits" sometimes took hold of the mediums. Three girls who became mediums for "reprobated spirits breathed nothing but hatred and blasphemy to God. They railed, they cursed, they swore, they heaped the vilest epithets upon the heads of the leaders, they pulled each other's and their own hair, threw knives, forks, and the most dangerous of missiles."

On one occasion I saw a sister inspired by a squaw, her head mounted with an old felt hat, cocked, jammed, and indented in no geometrical form, rush to a pan containing a collection of the amputated legs of hens, seize a handful of the raw delicacy, and devour them with as much alacrity as a yankee woman would an omelet or a doughnut. Hervey Elkins

At last the "gifts" began to die down, and "the degree of devotion in meeting depended more upon our own voluntary exertions than upon the aid of the communications from the spirit." Some Shakers even grew apologetic for the fervor, and the spirit drawings were buried in chests and cupboards. One by one the new rituals were abandoned. Believers who had always been devout continued their Shaker lives, and many others fell away.

Young sister.

Shocking apostacy! We learn this week that there has lately been a falling away at Hancock at the 2nd family, the like of which has scarcely been known before. Ten went away, four males and six females. They were chiefly between 15 and 22 years old. Some that had been visionists went, Elizabeth Oaks for one. Brother Isaac Youngs, 1839

Those who have learned that inspiration is not salvation, will not be surprised to learn that many of those who were seemingly most absorbed in the spirit work, finally became lukewarm and careless of their duties, and were at last swallowed up in the vortex of the world. Elder Henry Blinn

Flemming Eoff went to the world from the east house. He had been here 17 years, forty years old! Cupid must be hard pressed to swallow such bait as that! Shaker journal, 1859

I have known a time when going to the world seemed like the most awful step that anyone could take. At such times souls would bear admonition and mortification. But in such a time as this, when going to the world seems but little more to some than a walk into another room, they are in no condition to bear much admonition or to be restricted beyond what they think is just. Elder Freegift Wells

Business pressed hard, but few hands to do it. May we again be blessed with numbers more righteous than those we have lost. Philemon Stewart, 1847

Victorian ornament added to
a Shaker building, Canterbury.

8. TO THE END OF THE WORLD

Sabbath, February 1, 1863. At this time our minds are so much carried off with war and rumors of war that our spiritual travel is greatly impeded. Eldress Nancy Moore

Despite the increasing flow of members out of the societies, and the worldly values that prosperity had introduced into the societies, the Shakers still espoused isolation from the world and practiced it as best they could. They never voted or discussed politics, and insisted that the world's affairs were for the world's people. Even the great cause of emancipation, which the Shakers had instituted within their societies fifty years earlier, could not draw them into the Civil War. But the apocalyptic magnitude of the war made isolation impossible, even for the Shakers, and the transformation of America that followed it vitally affected the course of Shakerism.

Oh God! Protect this heritage from the ravages of cruel war. Elder's prayer

In the northern societies the effects at first had largely to do with enlistment. The diminishing numbers of new converts grew even smaller as men went off to war, and when the draft law of 1863 required *all* young men to register; even committed Shakers became eligible. So Elder Frederick Evans of Mount Lebanon put on his broad-brimmed hat and went to Washington to argue that the Shakers' pacifist principles should win them an exemption. He was received by Abraham Lincoln, who was very impressed with the articulate Shaker. "You ought to be made to fight," Lincoln told him. "We need regiments of such men as you." But he granted the Shakers an exemption from military service, making them among the first conscientious objectors.

As we look out of our windows, we see the western portion of our little village, to all appearance, a barrack for soldiers. The fires blazing, the sparks flying in high winds, their shouting and cheering contrast strongly with the quiet and peaceful appearance which has always characterized this place.

Eldress Nancy Moore

In the southern societies the impact of the war was much more direct. Union and Confederate troops often overran the villages, demanding food, supplies, and lodging, and stealing what was not given—blankets, grain, chickens, horses, anything that could be carried off. Often the Shakers were left without food or firewood for their own needs. At one point the Shakers at Pleasant Hill were feeding between three hundred and a thousand soldiers a day.

They surrounded our wells like the locusts of Egypt, and they struggled for water as if perishing with thirst. They thronged our kitchen doors begging for bread like hungry wolves. We nearly emptied our pantries of their contents and they tore the loaves and pies into fragments, devouring them. Shaker journal

Elder Frederick Evans, Mount Lebanon.

Limestone wall, Pleasant Hill.   The Shakers were always practical and economical in their
use of materials. Kentucky provided limestone rather than granite, and the villages looked
different accordingly. Despite varying materials, there was consistency throughout the villages,
reflecting the Shakers' striving for perfection in everything they did. These
particular walls are contemporary, but were built in the style of the original Shaker walls.

Sister Clarissa Jacobs. Embroidery and flowers, strictly forbidden in the first half of the nineteenth century, began to be popular at the turn of the century.

The Shakers were rarely reimbursed for their supplies, and were often vilified and threatened for not providing more. A lieutenant who was denied a fresh horse once railed, "You ought to be blowed out and the place destroyed. Here we are going night and day to protect you, and what in the Hell do you do for your country?" Any one of the desperate groups that passed through could have destroyed the villages, and the Shakers quietly prayed that no great harm would come to them. "Our head was in the lion's mouth," Elder John Eads said. "We had to be passive. Prudence would dictate nothing else."

At one time when Elder Solomon was tending sick soldiers, he was interrogated, as the brethren often are, about our religion. He quoted some scripture, and among the passages he added; the Savior says, if your enemy smite you on one cheek, turn to him the other. No sooner said, than one big, rough looking fellow popped him pretty keenly on the cheek; Elder Solomon involuntarily turned to him the other, he also slapped that without even a smile. Elder Brother passed it off pleasantly.

Eldress Nancy Moore

As the earth moves, the people must move with it, or be left in the rear. Elder Henry Blinn

. . . . . .

Important changes have taken place in the internal character of Shakerism; its leaders are more liberal and tolerant than they were half a century ago; more ready to see good in other systems, and less prompt to condemn what does not accord with their own.

William Hinds, 1902

The Shakers always considered themselves progressive people, always welcomed innovations if they saved time, simplified labor, increased health, reduced expenses, or otherwise improved life. The ability to accept change was an attribute that the Shakers cultivated, and members were frequently moved from room to room or job to job to teach them flexibility. "Progression," a Shaker wrote, "is one of the prominent points of our religious faith." But Shaker progress was always firmly grounded in certain unchanging principles: order, utility and simplicity, union and obedience, celibacy and separation from the world. These principles maintained the essence of Shakerism, so that its superficial aspects could fully adapt to the times.

But following the Civil War, industrialization, the growth of cities, and the loss of the frontier accelerated the pace of that progress beyond the Shakers' ability to adapt. Shaker hand labor, which had always been at the heart of the Shakers' religious practice, could no longer compete with machine-made goods. It became cheaper for the Shakers to buy things than to make them, and a weakening of the Shaker perfectionism and work ethic crept in with the parcels and packages. As worldly goods became increasingly acceptable, so did worldly values. As the Shaker population continued to diminish, there were fewer and fewer hands to do the work. Outside laborers had to be hired, increasing the worldly influences on formerly isolated Believers.

The sisters have taken a little more care for the ornamental. In one room the table was so filled with trinkets and pictures that we were strongly impressed to regard it as a showcase. Believers are noted for the large number that they possess, and a free exhibition gives all the pleasure of seeing the many beautiful, useless things that we hold in possession. Shaker journal

The appearance of Shaker rooms and buildings, and even of the Shakers themselves, began to change as asceticism yielded to materialism. Even the most conservative members, who felt that strict isolation from the world and its temptations was only way to save Shakerism, found themselves helpless against the tide of the times. The standards that had previously defined a Shaker softened in the new America.

With so much called into question, the door was open to a vanguard of Shaker leaders, for whom progress had a radically new meaning. These men and women felt that it was time to bring the virtues of Shakerism out into the world, to apply their principles to the whole of humanity. The future, they insisted, lay in joining forces with social reformers the world over. Old ways could not be held sacred if they were impeding progress.

A sect looks back, a church looks forward. The highest aspirations of the former never ascend above the measure of its founders, while those of the latter reach to God by an endless progression, through the means of continual revelation. Elder Frederick Evans

A disturbing element that has come into the societies is the free-thinking and infidel teachings of Elder F. W. Evans. I once heard him

Top: Shaker sisters. Hairdos without caps, dresses without bibs, in a room with plants and paintings and clutter, make these turn of the century sisters hardly identifiable as Shakers.

Bottom: Sitting room, trustee's house, Hancock. Visitors to a Shaker village were received in the trustee's house. The building was the place where Shakerism intersected the world, and it usually looked more worldly than the rest of the village. At the end of the nineteenth century, the trustee's house at Hancock was decorated like a Victorian parlor.

Trustee's House, Hancock.

Elder Harvey Eads, South Union, Kentucky.

Eldress Anna White, Mount Lebanon.

Elder Frederick Evans, Mount Lebanon.

say in a public discourse that he believed in the bible, and that he also believed in the dictionary! Brother Henry Cummings

Frederick Evans was an English radical who had come to America in 1820 with the Owenites in search of a perfect community. He was a well-traveled, well-read intellectual with firm ideas about social reform. For ten years he published political papers in America advocating abolition, the rights of man to the soil, equality for women, free public schools, and an end to wage slavery and imprisonment for debt.

In 1830 he visited the Shakers and was surprised to find that these people, whom he had once considered "the most ignorant and fanatical people in existence," were instead "religionists who were also rationalists, ready to render a reason for the faith and hope that was in them, and willing to have that reason tested by the strictest rules of logical ratiocination." His cathartic conversion came not with a vision of Jesus, or Ann Lee, or angels in heaven, but by a "mental phenomenon."

I could see a chain of problems as in a book, all laid out before me, starting from a fact which I did believe, and leading me step by step, mathematically, to a given conclusion which I had not hitherto believed. I then discovered that I had powers within me that I knew not of. I was reasoning as I never before reasoned.
Elder Frederick Evans

Evans became the most prominent Shaker who ever lived. He corresponded with reformers and politicians, published a Shaker newspaper, and lectured publicly on social issues. He encouraged Believers to educate themselves about world events, to read newspapers and magazines, and to study books on history, travel, and science. Union meetings became talks on subjects ranging from the beauties of the Bible to the proper use of irregular verbs, notes on Ireland, and postal laws. "Our little circle," one Shaker commented, "is quite an improvement over the sleepy, dull union meeting where conversation was turned out by machinery which had no motive power but a rusted, creaking crank." The Shakers began growing flowers, hanging pictures, and playing organs and even saxophones. Door sheds became porches, roof lines sprouted Victorian carvings, linoleum carpets covered polished floors. "Saints," Elder Frederick argued, "are as deserving of the good things of this world as sinners."

The Shaker may change his style of coat, may alter the cut of her gown or cease to wear a cap, and no harm be done. Vital harm may be done by retaining either, merely to preserve old forms and customs, when the time is crying out in vain for action; for spontaneous out-reaching sympathy here, aid there, cooperation yonder.

The international peace conference organized and hosted by the Shakers at Mount Lebanon in 1905. Two sisters with saxophones, Canterbury.

FIT Shakerism to humanity today, as the fathers and Mothers of the past fitted it to their age and time.   Eldress Anna White

Anna White was a brilliant and articulate leader in the late nineteenth century who took a less radical position on the question of what truly made a Shaker. She felt that intellectual flexibility and participation in the world's affairs were necessary to keep the Shakers in the modern age, but she firmly held that the covenantal principles were inviolate and that the spiritual life was still the essence of Shakerism. Eldress Anna belonged to the Women's Suffrage Association and was vice-president of the National Council of Women. She lectured on the rights of labor, the protection of animals, and peace. In 1905 the Shakers at Mount Lebanon held a universal peace conference with delegates from around the world. They called for reduced arms and taxes, an international police force, and a world court. White took the resolutions to Washington, where she was received by President Theodore Roosevelt. It was said that his eyes never wavered from Anna's piercing look. It was, as one observer noted, "Turk meets Turk."

It is a day of great improvements in the world,

a day of much free thinking and freedom of investigation, every many may judge for himself, and this spirit insinuates itself powerfully among the Believers, which is very injurious to their advancement in the gospel.

Brother Isaac Youngs, 1860

The characteristics of the soldier are developed in tents and on hardtack, not in gilded parlors or rich oyster saloons and ice cream pantries. Therefore it is our judgment that some fastings and mortifications of the body are commensurate with the greatest good.   1868

There was also a vocal and articulate conservative force in Shakerism, led by Elder Harvey Eads of Kentucky, that vigorously opposed the new trends and appealed for a return to the asceticism and isolation of the earlier days. But that course, regardless of its merits or faults, was impractical. The power of the encroaching world was beyond the Shakers' control. The call of the conservatives was against the flow of the times, it had a grave and sometimes ominous tone, and it required sacrifices that fewer and fewer Believers were willing to make. The decline continued.

Improvement in housing, schools, streets and sewers, the opening of railroads and mines, and

cities absorbing huge masses of humanity from all the nations of the world, these were the tasks which he, the Man of America, found awaiting him. The question of his soul's salvation or the gaining of heaven became absurdly irrelevant.   Eldress Anna White

We Americans love liberty too much to join such societies as these. What are they but pure despotism, where all are subject to the will of one man, a few leaders, or even a woman? Are not these places opposed to science and to all improvements? We Americans are a go-ahead people, not to be confined anywhere, or stopped by anything.   John Finch

Shaker population in 1860—5,200
1874—2,400
1891—1,700
1900—1,350
1910—1,000

In 1916 a friend sat with the old eldress of Harvard Shaker village and asked her, "Where has all the fervor gone, and all the spiritual fire that swayed these men and women? The wind of the spirit has swept through this place and borne the soul of it away on its wings. Only the outer shell of what was here remains to designate the spot through which it passed."

"Yea, oh yea," the eldress answered her. "Times have changed, and life is looked at from a different angle. But nothing that has gone before is lost. The spirit has its periods of moving beneath the surface, and after generations pass, it sweeps through the world again, and burns the chaff and stubble."

1908	Shirley, Massachusetts, closed
1912	Union Village, Ohio, closed
1917	Enfield, Connecticut, closed
1918	Harvard, Massachusetts, closed
1922	South Union, Kentucky, closed
1923	Enfield, New Hampshire, closed

By 1925 only six societies remained. The others had shrunk, consolidated, and finally closed. Some villages went into private hands, some became museums, some became prisons. Those still open were plagued by arson, run down by disuse and disrepair, and diminished by the death of males. Yet the twentieth-century Shakers quietly persisted, even as they became increasingly elderly and overwhelmingly female. They sold herbs and fancy goods in their village stores, tended bees and gardens, sang and worshiped sedately. In 1961 Elder Delmer Wilson of Sabbathday Lake, died. He was the last covenanted male Shaker, and shortly after his death the surviving eldresses decided to close Shakerism to new members forever.

December, 1889.   I'm sorry to hear of the loss of Groveland, and to hear that North Union must be broken up. The question very naturally arises, which society next?

August, 1890.   Society meeting. Sorrowful, pitiable sight. Few, say half a dozen children in the meeting circle. All, or nearly so dressed as worldly as possible. Can hardly be told as Shakers. Only three men dressed in Shaker costume.

Above: Canterbury.

Opposite: Dwelling, Canterbury.

Meetinghouse,
Pleasant Hill.

*A sympathetic public is prone to pity us and deplore the passing of the Shaker homes
as proof that Shakerism has failed. We are not depressed. It is all in the process of evolution.
Shakerism was founded on revelation and truth, and is progressive. The material homes
may fail, but the good lives on forever.*   Eldress Emma King

Doorway and chair,
center family dwelling,
Pleasant Hill.

Regardless of our numbers or our age, we have what the world is seeking and it will yet come into its own. What God has made alive will not stay buried. Sister Mildred Barker, 1967

Built-in cupboard,
Hancock.

A new age of spirituality is at hand, and the conditions now existing in embryonic form in the old-time Shaker communities will develop in a manner perhaps as startling to the Shakers as to the world. Conditions suited to the needs of the age will develop. The Shaker faith and the Shaker life will, from their elastic nature, be ready to receive the impress of a newly revealed truth and expand in new forms. Eldress Anna White, 1904

EPILOGUE

Shakerism is the most successful communal experiment in America. It has endured for more than 200 years, has survived the rise and fall of the popularity of religion and the changing values of an industrializing world. It has endured poverty and prosperity. It has endured the ridicule of its practices, the closing of its villages and the loss of its membership. Today, only a single village remains open, with just a handful of members, and still Shakerism endures.

Shakerism is a genuine religion. In the time when it flourished, it held the promise of the knowledge of God and connected its members with an aspiration both ancient and modern. Shakerism was the successful practice of this eternal striving, and therefore it endures. The Shakers practiced charity and humility. They practiced loving the other as themselves. They practiced sacrificing greed and egoism. They cared for their bodies with good food, good air, hard work, and herbal medicine. They practiced pacifism and turning the other cheek. They honored women and blacks as equals in the sight of God. They were true Christians, and their example is as inspiring and relevant in the twentieth century as it was in the eighteenth.

Today, Shakerism endures, not through the active practice of thriving communities, but through the power of the spirit that has been left behind. Shakerism still speaks for the eternal striving of humanity toward God. It speaks through the buildings and furniture, photographs, writings, and music that the Shakers instilled with their spirit. Testament to this are the enormous crowds who visit the restored village sites every year, and the exorbitant prices that people will pay to own a piece of furniture crafted by Shaker hands.

We were very fortunate to have known some of the last Shakers. These women lived, since childhood, in the Shaker way, immersed in the struggle for godliness and surrounded by love. They inspired us with their simplicity and grace. They taught quietly, through their example. They were the manifestations of a teaching that has been fulfilled. We will miss them.

More love, more love,
The heavens are blessing,
the angels are calling,
Oh Zion, more love.

If ye love not each other,
in daily communion,
how can ye love God,
whom ye have not seen.

More love, more love,
alone by its power,
the world we will conquer,
for true love is God.

If ye love one another,
then God dwellth in you,
and ye are made strong,
to live by his word.

Shaker Hymn

ACKNOWLEDGMENTS

We wish to thank the many people who helped us to understand the Shakers, or at least to ask the right questions: Stephen Marini, who challenged us with his animated and provocative inquiries; Wendy Tilghman and Tom Lewis, for research and writing; Flo Morse, for generously sharing her own invaluable book, *The Shakers and the World's People;* Wendy O'Connell, Camilla Rockwell, and Shimon Malin for their precise and insightful guidance; June Sprigg, for her vast expertise; Bud and Darryl Thompson, for their unique perspective; and Ed Nickels, Jim Thomas, Helen Upton, Jacob Needleman, John Ott, Jerry Grant and Geoff Ward, for sharing their understanding.

For their work on the book itself, we wish first of all to thank Michael Hoffman, who originated and supported the project, Geoff Ward and Steve Dietz, editors, Lorraine Davis, archival photographer, Steve Baron, who managed the production, and most importantly, Wendy Byrne, exceptional designer. We also want to thank Ned Gray for perfect printing, Deborah Franzblau for counsel, Lovel Richardson for artwork and general support, and Don Emerick for good advice.

At the villages and museums we wish to thank Richard Kathmann and Janet Deranian at Canterbury Shaker Village, Craig Williams at the New York State Museum, Richard Reed at Fruitlands Museum, Viki Sand and Ann Kelly at the Shaker Museum, Beatrice Taylor at the Winterthur Museum, and Robert Meader, Bev Hamilton, Susan Markham, Larry Yerdon, and especially June Sprigg at Hancock Shaker Village.

For the invaluable contribution of their own vision, we are very grateful to Langdon Clay and Jerome Liebling.

Our deepest gratitude goes to the Shakers themselves, and especially Eldresses Bertha Lindsay and Gertrude Soule, whose very lives teach more about Shakerism than all of the books and photographs combined.

Most of all, we want to thank our daughters, Sarah Lucile, who was born during the making of the film, and Anna Lilly, born during the making of the book, for their patience.

CREDITS

Contemporary photographs were taken especially for this book by Ken Burns, Langdon Clay, and Jerome Liebling.

Ken Burns: 2, 4, 8, 10, 12, 17, 18, 19, 26, 41, 42, 45, 46, 47, 48, 49, 50, 54, 60, 64 *(both),* 66 *(bottom),* 69, 72, 73, 79, 82 *(right),* 83, 84 90, 92, 98, 101, 110, 116 *(bottom),* 117, 121, 122, 123, 124, 128.

Langdon Clay: 21, 30, 31, 34, 51, 52–53, 61 *(top),* 62, 63 *(left),* 65, 66 *(top),* 74, 78, 81, 82 *(left),* 86 *(both),* 88 *(both),* 95, 97, 102, 104, 109 *(both),* 114, 120.

Jerome Liebling: 22, 29, 33, 87, 112.

Historical photographs were culled from various collections, to which grateful acknowledgment is given.

Fruitlands Museum, Harvard, Massachussetts: 15 *(top),* 58 *(all),* 59.

Hancock Shaker Village, Massachussetts: 38, 40 *(bottom),* 43, 57, 70 *(both),* 75, 89 *(bottom),* 99 *(bottom two),* 103, 104, 106 *(top),* 107.

New York State Museum, Albany: 15 *(bottom),* 23, 28, 36, 39, 68 *(top),* 71 *(top),* 76, 94 *(bottom),* 99 *(top).*

Shaker Museum, Old Chatham, New York: 6, 7 *(top, left, bottom),* 13, 14, 16, 20, 35, 37 *(both),* 40 *(top),* 44 *(both),* 53, 55, 61 *(bottom),* 63 *(right),* 67 *(top),* 68 *(bottom),* 71 *(bottom),* 77 *(both),* 80 *(both),* 89 *(top),* 91 *(both),* 93, 94 *(top),* 100, 106 *(bottom),* 108, 115, 116 *(top),* 118 *(all),* 119 *(left).*

Shaker Village at Canterbury: 7 *(right),* 11, 67 *(bottom),* 119 *(right).*

United Society of Shakers at Sabbathday Lake, Maine: 56, 85 *(bottom),* 105, 111, 113.

Henry Francis du Pont Winterthur Museum Library, Delaware: 85 *(top),* 96.

BIBLIOGRAPHY

Andrews, Edward Deming. *Community Industries of the Shakers.* New York State Museum Handbook Number 15, 1933. (Reprint) Emporium Publications, 1971.

Andrews, Edward Deming and Faith Andrews. *Religion in Wood; A Book of Shaker Furniture.* Bloomington: Indiana University Press, 1982.

Andrews, Edward Deming. *The Gift to be Simple.* New York: Dover, 1940.

Andrews, Edward Deming. *The People Called Shakers.* New York: Dover, 1953.

Andrews, Edward Deming. *Visions of the Heavenly Sphere.* Charlottesville: The University Press of Virginia, 1969.

Andrews, Edward Deming. *Work and Worship Among the Shakers.* New York: Dover, 1974

Brewer, Priscilla. *Shaker Communities, Shaker Lives.* Hanover, New Hampshire: University Press of New England, 1986.

Elam, Sister Aida and Sister Miriam Wall. *History of the Shakers:* Education and recreation. Canterbury, New Hampshire.

Evans, Frederick W. *Autobiography of a Shaker and Revelation of the Apocalypse.* Glasgow, Scotland: United Publishing Co., 1888. (Reprint) Philadelphia: Porcupine Press, Inc., 1972

Filley, Dorothy M. *Recapturing Wisdom's Valley.* Albany, New York: Albany Institute of Art and History, 1975.

Foster, Lawrence. *Religion and Sexuality.* New York: Oxford University Press, 1981

Hayden, Dolores. *Seven American Utopias: The Architecture of Communitarian Socialism, 1790–1975.* Cambridge: The MIT Press, 1976.

Holloway, Mark. *Heavens on Earth: Utopian Communities in America, 1680–1880.* New York: Dover, 1966.

Lindsay, Sister Bertha and Sister Lillian Phelps. *Industries and Inventions of the Shakers: Shaker Music,* Canterbury, New Hampshire.

Marini, Stephen. *Radical Sects of Revolutionary New England.* Cambridge: Harvard University Press, 1982.

Morse, Flo. *The Shakers and the World's People.* New York: Dodd, Mead, 1980.

Neal, Mary Julia. *The Journal of Eldress Nancy, kept at the South Union, Kentucky Shaker Colony, August 15, 1861–September 4, 1864.* Nashville: Parthenon Press, 1963.

Neal, Julia. *The Kentucky Shakers.* University of Kentucky Press, 1977.

Nordhoff, Charles. *The Communistic Sects of the United States.* New York: Harper & Brothers, 1875. (Reprint) Dover, 1966.

Pelham, R.W. *A Shaker's Answer to the oft Repeated Question, "What would become of the world if all should become Shakers?".* Boston: Press of Rand, Avery, & Co., 1874.

Sears, Clara Endicott. *Gleanings from Old Shaker Journals.* Fruitlands Museum, 1944.

Sprigg, June. *By Shaker Hands.* New York: Alfred A. Knopf, 1979.

Testimonies of the Life, Character, Revelations and Doctrines of Mother Ann Lee and the Elders with Her, Through whom the Word of Eternal Life was Opened in this Day of Christ's Second Appearing, Collected from Living Witnesses, in Union with the Church. Albany, New York: Weed, Parsons & Co., 1888 (Reprint) AMS Press, 1975.

Thomas, Samuel W. and James C. Thomas. *The Simple Spirit.* Pleasant Hill Press, 1973.

White, Anna and Leila S. Taylor. *Shakerism, its Meaning and Message.* Columbus, Ohio: Press of Fred. J. Heer, 1904. (Reprint) AMS Press, Inc., 1971.

Whitson, Robley Edward. *The Shakers: Two Centuries of Spiritual Reflection.* New York: Paulist Press, 1983.

INDEX

Note: Page numbers in *italic* refer to photographs, those in roman type to references within the text.

The Shakers: Hands to Work, Hearts to God is based on the film of the same name by Ken Burns and Amy Stechler Burns, which can be ordered from PBS Home Video, (800) 752-9727.

Copyright © 1987 by Aperture Foundation, Inc. Text copyright © 1987 by Amy Stechler Burns. Photographs copyright © 1987 by Ken Burns, Langdon Clay, Jerome Liebling. Specific photo credits are listed on page 126 and are considered a continuation of this copyright page. All rights reserved under International and Pan-American Copyright Conventions. No part of this book may be reproduced in any form whatsoever without written permission from the publisher. Composition by David E. Seham Associates, Inc., Metuchen, New Jersey. Printed and bound in Hong Kong by South China Printing.

Library of Congress Catalog Number 87-070736
ISBN 0-89381-860-7

The staff at Aperture for *The Shakers* is Michael E. Hoffman, Executive Director; Steve Dietz, Editor; Geoffrey Ward, Contributing Editor; Donald Young, Managing Editor; Stevan Baron, Production Director; Barbara Sadick, Production Manager. Book design by Wendy Byrne.

Aperture Foundation publishes a periodical, books, and portfolios of fine photography to communicate with serious photographers and creative people everywhere. A complete catalog is available upon request. Address: 20 East 23rd Street, New York, New York 10010. Phone: (212) 598-4205. Fax: (212) 598-4015. Toll-free: (800) 929-2323. Visit Aperture's website: http://www.aperture.org

Aperture Foundation books are distributed internationally through:

CANADA: General/Irwin Publishing Co., Ltd., 325 Humber College Blvd., Etobicoke, Ontario, M9W 7C3 Canada. Fax: (416) 213-1917.

UNITED KINGDOM, SCANDINAVIA, AND CONTINENTAL EUROPE: Robert Hale, Ltd., Clerkenwell House, 45–47 Clerkenwell Green, London, United Kingdom EC1R OHT. Fax: 44-171-490-4958.

NETHERLANDS, BELGIUM, LUXEMBURG: Nilsson & Lamm, BV, Pampuslaan 212–214, P.O. Box 195, 1382 JS Weesp, Netherlands. Fax: 31-294-41-5054.

AUSTRALIA: Tower Books Pty. Ltd., Unit 9/19 Rodborough Road, Frenchs Forest, NSW, Sydney, Australia, 2086. Fax: 61-2-9975-5599.

NEW ZEALAND: Tandem Press, 2 Rugby Road, Birkenhead, Auckland 10, New Zealand. Fax: 64-9-480-1455.

INDIA: TBI Publishers, 46 Housing Project, South Extension Part-1, New Delhi, 110049, India. Fax: 91-11-461-0576

For international magazine subscription orders for the periodical *Aperture*, contact Aperture International Subscription Service, P.O. Box 14, Harold Hill, Romford, RM3 8EQ, United Kingdom. One year: $50.00. Price subject to change.

To subscribe to the periodical *Aperture* in the U.S.A. write Aperture, P.O. Box 3000, Denville, New Jersey 07834. Phone: (800) 783-4903. One year: $40.00. Two years: $66.00.

First edition

10 9 8 7 6 5 4 3 2

Left: Dormer window, center family dwelling, Pleasant Hill.